Michigan's Thumb Drive

Michigan's Thumb Drive

A ride around M-25
Michigan's Blue Water Highway

MICHAEL J. THORP

SouThorp Publishers
Flint, Michigan

Also by Michael J. Thorp, Published by SouThorp Publishers

The Great, Great Lakes Trivia Test: The who, what, where, when why, and how of Michigan

The Legend of the Abominable Huckleberry: or The Practically True Tale of how the Huckleberry Railroad Got Its Name.

Published by SouThorp Publishers, Flint, Michigan

Publisher's Cataloging-in-Publication-Data

Thorp, Michael J.

Michigan's Thumb Drive/ Michael J. Thorp.- Flint, Michigan: SouThorp Publishers, 2014. ; cm.

ISBN 978-0-9844975-1-5   0-9844975-1-X

Michigan-Thumb-History- Fire-Geology-Tour-Miscellanea. 2. Great Lakes (North America) –Miscellanea. I. Title

FIRST EDITION

Layout and design by Steven D. Kimbrell

Printed in the United States of America

For Ginny; my biggest fan and the only critic who matters.

Dear reader,

I love to tell stories, and that is how this book started; stories of people and places, of the past and the potential future. The story of people is history.

"Michigan's Thumb Drive" is a trip, a sort of travel guide through a magnificent region of Michigan. As a reporter for many years and a lover of history I ask questions, usually they start with why and how and where and when. I can't help myself, I follow stories that catch my interest.

Why did the founders of the little community on Lake Huron call it Port Hope?

Who might be the most important political figure to come out of Michigan's Thumb?

How did two great conflagrations change forever the landscape of the Thumb?

Where do names of communities like Tuscola and Quanicassee and Wahjamega come from?

One of the things you will notice about my writing style is the tangents! I get curious about a subject, and as you will see, I follow some stories, sometimes beyond the Thumb; to see how the story ends or continues.

What billionaire's fortune can be traced, at least a bit, to his father's beginning in the Thumb? I follow that story in this book.

How did a guy who built his own lighthouse with a telephone pole and an old street light change a Thumb community forever? I follow that too.

I've even found the unpublished firsthand account of a 13 year old boy on what happened to him and what he saw in the Great Fire of 1881. It is a hair-raising adventure that he told to his daughter many years later.

....A little part of this story is about me too, my family and life. So I get to tell some of the stories just because I want to.

So enjoy the stories, and please forgive me for taking you off on many tangents as I follow stories that pique my curiosity. My hope is that you will get curious and start to follow a few tangents of your own.

If you have more information on these stories please let me know. Plus, if you have other "Thumb" stories that you think should be told, send them to me at michaeljthorp.com.

Michael J. Thorp

Author of

"Michigan's Thumb Drive"

Contents

Forward:

Think of this book as a tour guide for the Thumb of Michigan. It's also a history of the Thumb, and Michigan, a geological survey, an insight into a culture, an introduction to the people, a look at settlement geography and a course in natural disaster, with a dash of pre-history.

Look at that map of Michigan's Thumb and you see names like Bird Creek, Milwaukee Creek, Wisner, Grindstone City and Bad Ax. There is a story here, a story of people, and hard work and hard luck; tales of opportunity and riches, and of failure and loss.

A ride around the Thumb, on M-25, Michigan's Blue Water Highway, is a trip through the history of Michigan and the nation. There are legends of presidents and war heroes, famous inventors and explorers, simple farmers and sophisticated Ivy League professors; it's all here in one trip around the Thumb.

Enjoy your Thumb Drive through a beautiful, unique and surprisingly remote landscape and discover what you can learn from just the names that appear on a map and how they got there.

"If you seek a pleasant peninsula, we have plenty to choose from"!

Michael J. Thorp

(Paraphrasing Michigan's State Motto)

"Si quaeris peninsulam amoenam, circumspice"

Introduction

When you look at a map of the world, the whole world, not a lot jumps out at you. You'll see the continents the poles and probably Australia. But perhaps the most recognized shape you pick out is the famous Michigan mitten, and looking even closer you'll see the Thumb.

You might pick out a boot like shape on the European continent, that would be Italy, but it's the shape of Michigan, the mitten, that catches the eye. Few places on earth are able to be described like Michigan's Thumb.

Michigan's Motto is, "Si quaeris peninsulam amoenam, circumspice", which is Latin for "If you seek a pleasant peninsula, look about you. And Michigan is a state of peninsulas. Think about it; there are the upper and lower peninsulas, the Garden Peninsula and Keweenaw Peninsula off the Upper Peninsula, and the Leelanau and Mission Peninsulas near Traverse City in the Lower Peninsula. No matter where you live in Michigan; you live on a peninsula.

Michigan's Thumb is also a peninsula, the third largest in the state, after the upper and lower peninsulas. It is surrounded on three sides by the Saginaw Bay and Lake Huron and more than 150 miles of shoreline. The Thumb of Michigan contains over 100 miles of rivers and streams, 51,000 acres of public recreation land, 49,000 acres of state game/wildlife areas and some of the most beautiful farm land anywhere.

As we take our Thumb Drive along the Blue Water Highway, which is M-25, we will stay mostly in three counties, Huron County, at the tip of the Thumb, Tuscola

County, along the shore of Saginaw Bay, and Sanilac County along the beautiful shore of Lake Huron. We'll also take a side trip to the interior of the Thumb, the center of the peninsula where most of the people live.

Chapter 1

Prepping the Drive

There are at least a couple of places that claim to be "The Gateway to the Thumb." Reese, on the Saginaw and Tuscola County line, and Unionville in Tuscola County both claim the moniker. But for me Flint has always been the Gateway to the Thumb.

My Dad, LaVerne "Jim" Thorp, was born and raised near Kingston in the Thumb, as was his father and mother. When he joined the U.S. Army in 1950 he got off the farm and into a foxhole in Korea. He met my Mom, Barbara DeGrow of Flint, on a train. She was on vacation travelling with a girlfriend and he was on leave. After his leave, and Mom's vacation, he went back to Korea for a second tour. When he finally returned home he married my Mom and moved to Flint, her hometown, to build a life and a family. I was born there a year later and began my love affair with the Thumb.

For the next 17 years of my life my brothers and sisters and I went from Flint to the Thumb every Sunday, spent weeks on the farm with my grandparents, cousins and uncles and aunts. Fishing at Cat Lake and at Saginaw Bay, smelt dipping near Port Sanilac, hiking along old railroad beds, weeding gardens and much more. I spent a lot of time riding around the Thumb.

In 1973 I began a career as a broadcaster working at WKYO 1360AM, Caro in the center of the Thumb.

In that job I traveled all over the Thumb to do remote broadcasts. I helped crown the "Sweetest Girl in the

World - the Sebewaing Sugar Queen, hosted the Tuscola County Bean Queen program and broadcast live from the Munger Potato Festival. I awarded the WKYO blanket to the winning horse at the Tuscola County Fair sulky races and entered a tobacco spitting contest in Cass City, that didn't work out so well. I did high school football and basketball play-by-play and travelled to communities all over the Thumb. Like the old Hank Snow song said, "I've Been Everywhere" in the Thumb. It is a fascinating place.

In 2011 a friend of mine, John Schmitt, who owns a travel agency asked me if I would be interested in co-leading a bus tour of the Thumb. I was always interested in travelling in the Thumb, and now he was going to bring me people to tell stories to. Of course I was going to lead the tour. That is really where the idea for this book came from.

My first book, "*The Great, Great Lakes Trivia Test-The who, what, where, when, why and how of Michigan*", was a series of questions about our state, just to see what you knew, and from my perspective, what you could learn from my fun trivia about Michigan. How did Port Austin get its name? An amazing story you won't believe (The answer is coming later in this book).Who was the first European said to have seen the Great Lakes? Where did the journey that ended with the discovery of the mouth of the Mississippi begin? How old was Michigan's youngest Governor? Looking for the answers? Check out "*The Great, Great Lakes Trivia Test.*"

In 2012 I co-hosted a radio show with one of my great friends, Johnny Burke. He liked my book and used it on his show for trivia questions. Johnny is the morning host of WHNN 96FM, licensed to Saginaw, Bay City and Flint. At that time he did what he called his "Shake Hands with Michigan Tour." He would broadcast his show for a week from different places in the State. He asked me to write some more questions and travel along with him as we broadcast from Mackinaw City, Benzie County, St. Ignace and Port Sanilac in the Thumb. I found a whole lot of interesting facts and stories about the Thumb that I hadn't heard before, and I, of course, saved them.

The Thumb is a unique and beautiful peninsula with farms, wildlife, a fishing industry, lumbering, mining, shipping and tourism; its summers are filled with sailing and swimming, camping and fishing, festivals like the "Cheeseburger in Paradise Festival in Caseville and the Fish Sandwich Festival in Bay Port.

The Thumb story is one of tragedy, struggle, wealth, immigrants, wilderness, family and opportunity. The way I will tell the story is with a drive on the Blue Water Highway, M-25 from M-15 in Bay City to I-69 in Port Huron.

But before we hit the gas, let's start at the beginning to set the stage.

Michener I'm Not

I've always loved the way James Michener started his stories. He started at the beginning of time, as volcanos erupted, and asteroids from space struck Earth, molten lava then water everywhere. It's how he tells a story. I had a Physical Geography Professor at the University of

Michigan-Flint who assigned Michener's *Centennial* to the class. Well actually, he assigned the first few chapters. He said it was the best description of the beginnings of earth he ever read. He also said we didn't have to read the entire book. Personally, I couldn't put it down.

So, I'm not going to start at the very beginning, even if it is a very good place to start. I'm going to start where we need to start, when thousands of feet of ice covered the Thumb and most of Michigan.

An Icey Thumb

Michigan was carved by ice and water. Glaciers covered the area that would become Michigan till about 13,000 years ago. Glaciers pushed earth, dragged boulders, scraped imbedded rock. It scraped a rock smooth near Cass City where Natives would leave a message to the future, 1,000 years in the future. We'll learn more about the Sanilac Petroglyphs later. Glaciers dug out Saginaw Bay and the Great Lakes, and left depressions that became lakes, huge lakes.

Those huge lakes created caves and eroded rock before they receded, leaving behind the rocky shore at and around Pointe aux Barques, that some call the Thumbnail. We'll visit this place too, a little later.

As the glaciers melted they dropped rock, stone and dirt, left ground sunken by the enormous weight of the glacier ice. Melt water flowed and filled those depressions. When the water had no place to go it drained haphazardly around glacial deposits and into the depressions. This created a strange drainage area, which is why there are no valleys or long deep rivers in the Thumb or in Michigan for that matter. Streams in the Thumb are what they call accidental and winding: rivers are short and there a many lakes and swamps.

A Pleasant Climate

Peninsulas are special environments. Surrounded by water the cold and heat are moderated. A story in Harper's Weekly in 1871 reported that Michigan's Thumb would be 3 degrees warmer in winter and 3 degrees cooler in summer, when compared with the middle of the state. The same article goes on to say that the Thumb is generally 6 degrees warmer in winter and 6 degrees cooler in summer than at the same latitude in Minnesota.

Winds are generally westerly, in the Thumb, which pushes sand up on its eastern shores. One of the few places on the east side of the state you'll find sand dunes is at Port Crescent State Park where Lake Huron meets Saginaw Bay. The most famous place in Michigan where those westerly winds push sand dunes is on the eastern shore of Lake Michigan at northwest Michigan's Sleeping Bear Dunes.

Thumb Dwellers & Visitors

The French first arrived in the Michigan country around 1620. They were traders, trappers and missionaries, some were called the Courier du bois, translated as woods runners; and they traveled all through the region, canoeing the lakes, rivers and streams. The first European to see Lake Michigan was a Frenchman; Jean Nicolet in 1634.

The French were known to give generous gifts and trade better goods to the Indians, they married into the Indian tribes, they were interested in trade only, and most importantly were NOT interested in the Indian land. So the French were much more welcome than the English who traded inferior goods, remained segregated from the Native People, and most threatening; they wanted the Indian land.

By around 1760 French sailors were traveling around the Thumb. They named the rocky outcroppings along the tip of the Thumb, Pointe aux Barques, because from the lake the rocks looked like "points of ship" moored along the shore.

But the French were not the first people in the Thumb. People had been living and visiting the Thumb for hundreds of years.

Thumb People

The first people in Michigan's Thumb followed the melting ice sheet around 12,000 years ago. They were trailing the mammoth and mastodons that were essential to their lives for meat, fuel, clothing and shelter. We don't know a lot about these people except that they likely hunted but did not stay in the Thumb year around.

As the climate in the Thumb warmed the Native population had to adapt. Their tools become more advanced, some built mounds, and tools like arrowheads and other stone tools. They began to hunt smaller animals as their spears became more accurate.

By the year 100 BCE the Hopewell culture, a woodland tribe began to spread around Michigan. They traded
with Native cultures from as far away as the Rocky
Mountains and the Gulf of Mexico. These Indians carved
drawing in stone, called petroglyphs. One of the few
known places in Michigan you can see petroglyphs is in
the Thumb. Faded and obscured the Sanilac Petroglyphs
still amaze, more about that later.

Then the more recent tribes came to the Thumb,
descendants of the first native peoples. These cultures
were a loosely based group referred to as the, "Three
Fires Confederacy."

The fires were the tribes; the Ojibwa, also known as
the Chippewa, who were the Keepers of the faith, the
Ottawa, also called the Odawa, the Trader People, and
the tribe most closely associated with the Thumb, the
Potawatami, or Bodwewadomi, Keepers of the Fire.

These peoples spoke an Algonquian language called
Anishinaabeowen and had no written language. Their
history was passed down by storytelling. The women
grew corn, beans, squash and rice helped by the long
growing season in the lower part of Michigan. The men
were hunters and fishermen. They stalked deer, birds,
bison, bear, turkey, elk and small game.

They lived in wigwams, not the kind of teepees you see
in old John Wayne movies. These wigwams were dome
shaped with walls made of cedar, elm and birch bark.
On the bottom of the outside walls, like a wainscot, the
women would weave reeds and grasses into the wall to
allow air to circulate. The doors of wigwams were east
facing, to meet the rising sun and were covered with
animal hide.

The Sauk and Fox tribes were known to live in what is now Saginaw. Many people think these were two parts of the same tribe. By 1734 they were described as one people. The Sauk called themselves Asa-ki-waki, which in the Algonquian language means people of the outlet. They had been gathering at the "outlet" since the early 1700's.

The outlet they were referring to was the Saginaw River's outlet into Saginaw Bay. The Sauk people gave their name to the land, Saginaw basically means place of the Sauk's.

Many place names around the Thumb remember the original settlers, Indianfields Township in Tuscola County is a memory of the Indian farms, Quanicassee, Sebewaing and Pinnebog too, and all are reminders of the first residents of the Thumb. We'll learn more about what those names mean, later in this story.

The Thumb By Any Other Name

The three counties in the Thumb, Sanilac, Huron and Tuscola, are all based on Indian names, sort of. Sanilac may be based on the Algonquin word "zngwak" which means pine. Other sources suggest Sanilac County, most likely, was named for Chief Sannilac, who was Wyandotte.

Huron County was named for the Indian tribe, which took its name from Lake Huron. The Hurons were the only non-Algonquian tribe in Michigan, they spoke an Iroquoian language. More places are named for this tribe than any other in Michigan.

There is a lot of controversy as to where the name "Huron" came from. Was it of French origin or native? The earliest known use of the word Huron was in 1634 when Father Paul Le Jeune wrote in *Jesuit Relations*, "that because the Indians wore their hair in ridges they looked like boars", or in French; hures, hence the name Hur-on.

Another theory is that the name is from Iroquois word Irri-non or Eries meaning cat nation. The French seemed to add an "H" to everything, so, the word Irri-non became, Hirri-non, or Huron. This story suggests that the name for Lake Erie and Lake Huron are two versions of the same word. No matter, Huron is another word derived from Native Americans.

Perhaps the most interesting name of all is Tuscola County. It was named by Henry Rowe Schoolcraft. He was a geographer, geologist, born in Albany County, New York in 1793.

Henry Rowe Schoolcraft

THUMB NOTE

Henry Schoolcraft was Michigan's first Indian Agent and an ethnologist who studied Native American cultures. In 1820, Schoolcraft served as a geologist on future Governor Lewis Cass' expedition along Lake Huron and Lake Superior, west to the Mississippi River, down the river to present-day Iowa, and then returning to Detroit after tracing the shores of Lake Michigan.

By 1822 Schoolcraft was an Indian Agent in Sault Ste. Marie, Michigan where he met and married Jane Johnston granddaughter of an Ojibwa chief named Waubojeeg. She shared her knowledge of the Ojibwa legends she learned as a girl with her husband. He wrote many studies about Native populations and the stories he learned from his wife became the source material for Longfellow's epic poem, The Song of Hiawatha, more on that later.

Jane Johnston Schoolcraft, was the first known Native American literary writer. She married Henry Rowe Schoolcraft. Her stories became Longfellow's "Song of Hiawatha."

He created the map of Michigan and it needed place names. Schoolcraft named places for members of the President's cabinet, and used Indian names he thought appropriate. But when he ran out of ideas he used a bit of creativity and just made some up. Names such as Alcona, Algoma, Allegan, Alpena, Arenac, Iosco, Kalkaska, Oscoda and Tuscola, for example are all from the ingenious mind of Henry Schoolcraft. Schoolcraft combined words and syllables from Native American languages with words and syllables from Latin and Arabic to invent new words.

Thumb Names

So Tuscola, sounds like a Native American word and looks like one, but it is not, it just sounded "Indian" to Schoolcraft. It is a "neologism"; a newly coined term, word or phrase that may be in the process of entering common use, according to a dictionary. Neologisms are often directly attributable to a specific person or publication.

Henry Schoolcraft loved creating new neologisms, and words he created, like Tuscola, are very common today.

On our Thumb drive we will learn about the beginning of many communities and how they were named. Many were named for people, others named for the place they are. But many were named for the first settlers of the area, the Native Americans and, as we have seen, there are many spellings of the words. The words can be hard to trace and spell.

In 1884 a teacher and writer from Massachusetts wrote a verse about Indian words in a poem called "On the Cape." Her poem was about the Native American place names on the east coast, but it also fits when talking about Michigan place names.

On the Cape
"We drove the Indians out of the land,
But a dire revenge those Redmen planned,
For they fastened a name to every nook,
And every boy with a spelling book
Will have to toil till his hair turns gray
Before he can spell them the proper way."
Eva March Tappan

Thumb Burns

Wherever you go in the Thumb of Michigan the echo of the great fires of 1871 and 1881 are evident. Those fires changed everything for those who survived; where they lived, what they did, what grew on their farms, what they feared and what they dreamed. You can't look at the Thumb and overlook the fires. So, let's talk about the fires.

Lumbering Changed Everything

Let's start by imagining what the great Thumb wilderness looked like before the fires. In 1800, the forests of the Thumb were thick with the ancient pine that would build Michigan and much of the country. White pine trees from Michigan rebuilt Chicago after the fire of 1871. What many don't realize is that the lumbermen of Michigan made more money, created more wealth, towns and businesses and had more impact than all the gold ever mined in California.

There was also hardwood trees like oak, maple, hickory, elm, beech, poplar, cedar, birch, hemlock, black cherry, elder; over 100 species of trees are native to Michigan and most of those were found in the forests of the Thumb.

The Thumb had vast swamps, rivers and streams that drained into Lake Huron and Saginaw Bay. Stories are told of how when you entered the forest of the Thumb you went into a world of twilight. Sun light seldom was able to reach the forest floor because of the canopy high above; it was a swampy, dark, dense forest-wilderness.

The forest protected the swamps, and kept the ground moist in the hottest of times

At the turn of the 19th Century the Thumb forest had great numbers of elk, deer, rabbit, bear, fox, wolf, cougar, badger, coyote, birds of all kind, fish and snakes, frogs, snails, and more. And don't forget the animal that brought the first European settlers, the beaver. In short, the forest wilderness of Michigan's Thumb was a quiet, dark place teeming with wildlife.

Native Americans had been living in the Thumb for hundreds of years living off the land, taking advantage of the wildlife, and the fish, and the forest wilderness to live. They moved with the season and the wildlife. They were a part of the forest, living within it.

Then the trappers arrived, mostly French-Canadians; they were known as the Courier de bois, or runners of the woods.

These woodsmen traveled in New France, which included Michigan to trade for furs, especially beaver pelts. They used the lakes and rivers as highways and began to open up the wilderness. They lived with the native people and learned their ways often taking an "Indian" wife. These strong, fearless entrepreneurs explored, trapped and traded but did not change anything they found. In many ways they lived like the native people they traded with.

After 1800, as the French were driven out, the trappers were now the Americans who had travelled west to make their fortune. They founded settlements like Flint and Saginaw so they could sell their pelts for food, equipment and whiskey. Soon the beaver disappeared from the Thumb and a different kind of entrepreneur came, he was eyeing the forest itself.

By 1835 the first steam mills appeared on the Saginaw River, within 20 years 23 steam mills were situated on the just the Saginaw River alone. Mills were everywhere consuming the forest as fast as it could be brought to the saw. Michigan's 14th Governor, Henry H. Crapo, born in 1804, came to Michigan in 1858 from his native Massachusetts and bought thousands of acres of forest for the lumber. He built the Flint and Holly Railroad, which later became the Flint and Pere Marquette Railroad, to bring lumber from the Thumb forests. Arthur Hill in Saginaw was also buying land and cutting the trees.

There was a lot of money in the wilderness of Michigan and men wanted it.

And the virgin forest trees were huge. At the 1876 Worlds Fair in Philadelphia, PA a board that was cut somewhere between Harbor Beach and Bad Axe was a featured exhibit from Michigan; it was 16 feet long and 4 feet wide. Stumps that were 8ft in diameter and larger were reported.

By 1851 much of the pine and hardwood had been cut from the Thumb forest, but that wasn't the worst of it. Lumbermen were careless with what they called "slashings." Slashings were the pine tops, the branches, leaves, pine needles discarded trunks of trees that were left on the forest floor. The lumbermen only wanted the tallest and straightest trunks; that's where the cash was. So the refuse was left to dry. In some areas the slashings were 12 to 15 feet high, covering thousands of acres.

By 1872 100 million feet of logs was taken from the

Cass River area alone. As the forest was felled and taken the ground dried up, the moist forest became a hot dry plain. Streams dried up, or were filled with refuse and polluted. Swamps were drained and dried up, the landscape of the Thumb changed forever from that cool, dark, swampy, dense forest to a landscape of dead tree trunks and wood scraps. Much native game disappeared, and so did fish and many species of birds.

This is what the Thumb wilderness looked like on the eve of the great fires!

Chapter 2

Raging Infernos

The Great Fire of 1881

By September of 1881 the forest was a tinderbox. The summer of 1881, had been one of the hottest and driest in anyone's memory. There had been no significant rain since June. Sgt. William Bailey, Station Manager of the U.S. Signal Corp office in Port Huron, believed the fire started on August 31 in Lapeer County along the south branch of the Cass River into Marlette. But there were a lot of fires. The smell of smoke and wood burning had become common for weeks.

What about all those fires people were reporting, where did they come from? The answer is local farmers

Illustration by August Kimbrell

set them. After much of the lumber had been taken lumbermen no longer had use for the land, so it was sold, cheap, in 40, 80 and 160 acre parcels. This land had been cleared of valuable lumber and left covered with the slashing and stumps, huge stumps. The land resembled a vast wasteland, but under it all the soil was good for farming if farmers could get to it.

Removing stumps that could be as much as 8 feet in diameter was a huge feat of strength as they had to be dug out by hand. The slashings were 12-15 feet high in some areas.

To clear the land farmers had to dig stumps and cut up piles of slashing, which could take years for a small farmer who was working a 40 or 80 acre plot with no one to help but his family. And while he dug out he couldn't plant crops, which is how he was feeding his family. There had to be an easier way!

There was; the same method we use today when we are cleaning out property, a burn. Farmers all over the Thumb burned huge piles of slashing and stumps. All summer long they burned. Of course things burn better and quicker when it is dry, so they were taking advantage of the dry weather to clear their land. Today, of course, we have to get a permit to burn outdoors in most communities. That is a vestige of the great fires of 1881.

The *Saginaw Daily Courier* reported on September 6, 1881 that, "at 2:15 this morning the fire could be distinctly seen from Genesee Avenue looking eastward." A letter in the September 7, 1881 *Bay City Tribune* said, "The Thumb is as dry as a man after eating salt mackerel." According to stories sailors on ships sailing up Lake

Huron could see small fires everywhere and smoke was so thick that they were sounding the fog horn.

The fires moved fast. They started to converge when a huge windstorm kicked up. On September 1 a fire reached Sandusky, burning a school and house.

It exploded in the swamp of the Black River, crossed the river and hit Deckerville. By September 3 it reached Carsonville, on September 4th the fire was burning fields on the Mackinaw Road, 2 miles from Saginaw.

Children in Cass City went to School that morning but soon were dismissed because of the dense smoke. Fire had been smoldering for days in that area. According to Sgt. Bailey, strong winds rose and, "hundreds of fires were burning in the Thumb and within an 8 mile radius of Cass City, "every house save one was burned."

Still, according to the stories of the time; people went about their business, thrashing grain, plowing fields, heading to town, mailmen delivering, livestock being tended to, and farmers burning brush.

By this time, ten miles west of Bad Axe, the fire was out of control. Roderick Park wrote, in the *Thumb Fire of 1881*, "In Bad Axe the haze of the white smoke and odor of burning brush left the sun a red ball in the sky, hot, dry." The heat was sweltering and the parched baked landscape was hard as a rock, the acrid smell of the burning forest was everywhere, the smoke hung heavy over land and lake.

Old timers were reminding anyone who would listen that the sun looked as it had for weeks before the great fire of 1871, yes, it had happened before.

October 8, 1871 "The Day Michigan Burned"

Ten years earlier there had been another horrifying conflagration. It was so bad that October 8, 1871 was known simply as, "the day Michigan Burned", but Michigan wasn't the only place that burned.

The summer of 1871 was, just as 1881, hot, dry and parched. No significant rain had fallen in months, farm fields had dried up with crops wilted and dead. This drought did not just affect Michigan; it was felt throughout the Midwest. It wouldn't take much to set the disaster off.

Many have heard the story of Mrs. O'Leary's cow. The story goes that Mrs. O'Leary went out to milk her cow in the City of Chicago when the cow kicked over her lamp starting the fire that consumed much of the great city. Another theory was a comet, yes a comet. Mel Waskin suggested in his book, *Mrs. O'Leary's Comet,* that a comet struck earth raining "fiery particles" down on Chicago, Wisconsin and Michigan. Lightening was also blamed. Many today believe that it was just the hot, dry summer and a huge windstorm that was the key

Arguments have raged for over a century as to which, if any, of these stories are true. In the end it doesn't matter; a fire was lit and over 1,500 died in Chicago and Wisconsin. The city of Peshtigo, Wisconsin was all but destroyed and hundreds lost their lives.

The fire of 1871 burned into the Upper Peninsula of Michigan, likely set by ash and sparks that were blown over the Menominee River by gale force winds from Wisconsin.

Ash and embers from Chicago may have set Holland, Michigan ablaze that day. Manistee and Glen Haven were destroyed. Fires fanned by tornado-like winds spread all along the west coast of Michigan, along the lake. Fires were burning as far north as the Au Sable River in Lower Michigan.

In Michigan the worst hit areas though were in the Thumb forests. The focus was a 40 square mile area between Saginaw Bay and Lake Huron. The Thumb was even more wilderness then than in 1881. No accurate record of the losses was ever made, but the estimates are that at least 200 people in Michigan lost their lives in the Great Fire of 1871, hundreds of families lost their homes and two million acres of land "burned over."

I used the term "burned over" specifically because the way the fire burned in 1871 set the stage for what happened in 1881. The fire of 1871 was called a "tree top" fire. That means that this fire burned off the tops of the trees, killing them but leaving them standing, dead, drying and decaying. The fire burned over swamps and left dry refuse.

It didn't burn the slashings off it just left even more dead, dry refuse. The 1871 fire simply killed the trees; it did not consume them; that was left to the Great Fire of '81.

The Great Fire of 1871 ended with a huge rainstorm, the first in months; just a day after the fires had "burned Michigan".

The 1871 fire was the beginning of the end of the lumbering industry in the Thumb forests. Much of the lumber had been taken and most of what was left was killed in the fire. Thereafter lumbering was limited to small patches of forest that remained and finding trees left after the fire. The lumbermen continued to strip the trees and leave the slashings to the forest.

In 1871 it was careless lumbering, an intense drought and, most significantly, tornado and gale force winds that drove the fire across the City of Chicago, which was mostly made of wood, across the lake and into the forests of Michigan and Wisconsin. It drove the fires to high heat and intensity and destroyed much in its path. The Great Fire of 1871 was, like a shot across the bow, a warning of things to come.

Phenomenons of the Fire

The stories of the Great fire of 1881 are horrific, sad, scary and amazing.

Weather and fire phenomena can make a fascinating study. Fire affects the weather and weather effects fire.

Howling Wind

Fires were burning for weeks before the fire really took off in 1881. Farmers used fire to clear fields of slashings and brush. Small fires, some that were barely under control, were everywhere. On September 10, 1881 the *Detroit Free Press* reported, "The wind fanned the existing fires and soon drew walls of flame across the land. Horses that galloped before the flames were overtaken by them and left roasting on the ground."

High winds, gale force winds, tornados drove the fires. Some of the gusts were reported at 40-60 miles per hour. The wind was part of a weather pattern, but the fire also pushed the wind as it swept up land, trees, homes, livestock, wildlife and people. Wind that blew roofs off of barns and houses, winds that blew men and women off the ground, rolled large boulders and knocked down large trees.

A Mighty Roar

The wind was roaring; that was the word witnesses used, roaring. It was so loud that people had to yell to be heard, and that was before the fires reached them. The winds fanned the flames, building the fire, the roar of the forest being consumed with huge explosions.

On Monday September 5, 1881 it was reported that there was a "tremendous roar" an explosion that sounded like artillery west of Harbor Beach. It was the sound of the fire exploding.

Black as Midnight

Also on Monday the *Huron Times* reported, "A strange darkness, black as that of midnight, settled on the devoted village of Sand Beach (now Harbor Beach). Indeed, without exaggeration, it was impossible to see one's hand before one's face." One writer said that many believed it was an eclipse and were checking their almanacs, it wasn't.

People were said to have watched to the west as miles of burning material made the western sky red with the heat and flame, but no sunlight could break through... at 4:30 in the afternoon. It was so dark that afternoon that Richmondville, MI. Postmaster F. Murray reported the street lamps were lit and people were forced to light their lanterns. In the *Portrait and Biographical Album of Sanilac County-1884* one report said, "It went from dark to a billow of fire that rushed upon them from out of the darkness and enveloped whole towns almost in the twinkling of an eye."

On the east coast of the United States signs of the inferno could be seen in the sky. Boston, MA newspapers reported, "Strange yellowish skies to the west", Smoke and ash were said to have obscured the sun over that city for several hours.

It was black as midnight, hot as hades, dry as a desert, and so much smoke that you couldn't breathe or see on a September Monday afternoon.

Great Balls of Fire

Then the fire balls began to fly. Large and small, fireballs fell ahead of the wall of fire. In his book, *The Thumb Fire of 1881*, Roderick Park described this as, "a strange phenomenon where flames would leap into the sky and then descend to the ground bouncing like a ball, destroying everything, and then bouncing up again."

In Richmondville they started seeing balls of fire. The glowing balls fell all over the town destroying everything except the local hotel and one abandoned house. Villagers who survived were in the lake, some suffocated when the fire consumed all the oxygen.

Candles in the Wind

Another curious phenomenon reported by several observers, a strange blue-white flame would sometimes burst forth from tree stumps. Witnesses said it looked like a candle. The flame appeared in stumps that were left from the 1871 fire.

The flame was caused by the incredibly high temperature of the fire that set fire to stumps left from the Great Fire of 1871.

These stumps, which had been half burned ten years earlier, were essentially now charcoal. These stumps would flame up like a candle then with a gust of wind would be blown out like a candle.

On the Lake

Many lives were saved, animal and human, by taking to Lake Huron. For weeks sailors had reported glowing fires along the shore. Foghorns were blaring because ship captains couldn't see through the smoke. The heat and glow of the fires could be seen and felt 7 miles out on the lake.

At Grindstone City fires burned for days. Two schooners, the Trojan and the Wilcos were lying on the dock ready to save the people if the fire got that far, it didn't.

At Huron City, according to Sgt. Bailey, "The fire became a whirlwind. It raced through the settlement and headed for Port Hope." At Port Hope the schooner Lamb caught fire at the dock. The propeller, City of Concord tied a line and hauled the Lamb out into the lake to put out the fire. The City of Concord then took a number of residents to safety in Port Huron. Captain Hebner, of the City of Concord, reported that the shore from Port Sanilac to Port Austin was, "One sheet of flame."

Taming the Beasts

There are accounts of people who jumped into lakes and rivers to save themselves from the firestorm all over the Thumb. They would be there in the pitch black and when they finally could see their surroundings they realized they were with wild animals, black bears who seemed to have a need to be with humans in this awful danger, wolves, fox, deer. It was said that there was no fear of the animals; it was, according to some observers, as if a truce had been called between man and beast.

It wasn't just in water, but in the fields where some ran to avoid the infernos. The people would wake up to find that they were surrounded by wild animals also looking for a place to survive.

Some tales of the fire recall how the first warning of the blazes was the rustle of many, many wild animals fleeing for safety. Rabbits, squirrels, voles, birds of all feathers, deer, all racing to beat the flames.

Winds of Mercy

Wind does strange things; it can come up fast and disappear in an instant. Wind can cool you when it's hot and push a wall of flames miles in minutes. During both the great fires wind was the cause, but sometimes the wind was a lifesaver.

Port Austin, at the tip of the Thumb was saved by the wind. For hours the fire was bearing down on the little village, pushed along by huge gusts of gale force winds. Then, just as things looked lost a strong wind from the north blew the fire away from the town and into Lake Huron.

It was reported that Sand Beach, (now Harbor Beach) was saved from the fire by a sudden east wind. The same thing happened inland, winds would kick up and blow the fire over a house, sometimes the wind would force the fire to split and everything to the left and right of a building would be completely destroyed, but in the middle, like an island in the stream, would be a house or barn standing safe in the midst of carnage.

The wind caused by the fire, and the natural winds from the storm began a battle which only brought more destruction. In Minden, (now Minden City) the wind from the northwest and southwest tangled to cause what was described as a terrible noise, "like the roaring of mighty waters." These are the winds that save the town.

Blossoming of the Trees

The heat of the fires withered leaves on trees two miles and more away, fields of potatoes, onions and corn not touched by the flame were roasted on the vine and in the ground.

Survivors were said to have eaten fully cooked potatoes right out of the ground.

One of the strangest things reported after the fires was the pear, apple and other fruit trees that were said to have strange growth and to have actually blossomed again.

Chronicals of Fire

A few other stories related by witnesses of the Great Fire of 1881.

Hillside Cemetery is a lonely place; it seems like it is out in the middle of nowhere. Hillside, also called Southerland and Wheatland Cemetery, was built on barely one acre of land is a memorial to the Great Fire of 1881.

The cemetery is located three miles east and one mile north of Argyle, in Michigan's Sanilac County and is contained completely by the Minden City State Game Area.

It was started when local lumberman and farmer John Cole, who was born in Rosehill, Virginia in 1840, discovered the bodies of the six right after the fire.

The cherry tree & marker

He and his wife, Susan Seder Cole buried the six victims on land they donated from their nearby 1866 homestead. After the burial Mr. Cole planted 3 cherry trees close together to mark the grave.

Today those cherry saplings have grown together, intertwined into an impressive triple Cherry tree that still marks the grave of;

Emma Palmer, 52.

Neil Erhart, 30.

Mary Ann Erhart, 24.

Clara Howard, 8.

William Erhart, 2.

Clara Erhart, 9 days.

The stone marker with the names of the victims was placed in the late 1950's.

This is just one of the graves, one of the tragic stories, among dozens, of victims of the Great Fire of 1881.

John and Susan Seder Cole are also buried in the cemetery along with just over 200 others.

Their children placed a marker in the cemetery in their memory. It said;

Erected by their children most of whom were born on this farm 40 rods south of this point. William J., Nelson J., John M., Jr., Melvin R., Mary E., Ella J., Jennie M., George A., Caroline E., James F., Harriet B., Myrtle M., Lucy A., Winfred J.

"Cole, John M. and his wife, Susan Seder Cole, pioneer settlers who homesteaded this farm in 1866 and started this cemetery by finding and burying victims of the forest fire Sept. 5, 1881. John was a Union soldier, serving in 61st NY Vol. Inf., Co. E, 8th Mich Cav, Co. G."

Railroads

Fires were reported on and near railroad tracks all over the Thumb. The line to Bad Axe was closed; engineers reported steaming through flames on both sides of the tracks. Some trains cars were burned on the tracks.

Fire was reported along the Flint & Pere Marquette Railroad. The *Detroit Evening News* reported on September 6, 1881 that, "between Bridgeport and the Birch River the fires are bad and the village of Clio was threatened." Freeland was threatened, in Seidens three miles of fire was reported.

Men working on the Saginaw, Tuscola & Huron Railroad bed were driven off by the fire. On a train, there was no place to run or hide.

Lighthouse

 On Monday, September 5 the wind kicked up and the fire flared and roared toward the Pointe aux Barques Life Saving Station, which was just 300 yards from the lighthouse, which still stands. The Keeper of the light, Andrew Shaw and all his hands fought the fire and saved the lifesaving station and the lighthouse.

They took all flammables to the lake, took anything they needed, to the lake and started filling anything they could with water. They kept the lighthouse and station as wet as they could for hours on end and saved the light the station and equipment.

Keeper Andrew Shaw

Mr. Shaw's farm, less than a mile away, was reduced to ashes. Andrew Shaw was appointed Lighthouse Keeper at Pointe aux Barques by Abraham Lincoln in 1863. Born in Dublin Ireland in 1824, he and his crew saved the light from the Great Fire.

Bad Axe

The Town of Bad Axe was hit hard by the fires as they converged on the area. More buildings were lost in that town than in any other. 400 people survived the horror by staying in the newly built brick courthouse. At 7a.m. on Tuesday September 6 a Charles Thompson reported it was 110 degrees inside the courthouse because of the fire. The people inside the courthouse slept on hardwood floors in hunger as they watched their town burn around them.

Fire Everywhere

"Fires between Caro and Vassar destroyed much property", the *Vassar Times* said on September 8, 1881.

The report went on to say, "the fire of 1871 was a bonfire compared to this." Clare, Isabella, Gratiot, Genesee, Lapeer, Tuscola, St. Clair Counties were all affected. The further north and east in the Thumb you went, the more devastation was seen.

Trains were held up, the telegraph lines down; communities of the Thumb completely cut off from the outside world.

Many stayed in the Cass River for hours to dodge the fires. Sometimes the fire crossed the river right over them. The river got so hot that it cooked the fish in the river, killing thousands.

The fire was so hot that, in a letter to the brand new American Red Cross, a J.B. Hubbell said, "Men and women, cattle hogs and horses were burned to death in open farm fields hundreds of feet from the fire."

The Clothes Off Your Back

You've heard the saying that, he was so good he would give you the shirt off of his back if you needed it. In the Great Fires of 1881 many, if not most of the people lost everything they owned; house, barn, family, livestock, farm equipment, tools, business and even the clothes on their back.

In another of those strange stories there were dozens of reports of people wandering around completely naked. Their clothes literally burned off their back. In some cases they had stripped off their clothes when they caught fire.

The Flames Die

The fires in the Thumb forests burned till there was nothing left, and consumed everything in its path; in some places it burned itself out. But, just like the fires of 1871 it smoldered till, once again just like in 1871, a heavy rain on Wednesday September 7th, the first in months, doused most of the flames.

The awful toll, at least 282 dead, many unidentified,

15,000 homeless and hungry, 3,400 buildings confirmed destroyed, 2,000 square miles burned, business' and families destroyed, crops laid to waste, thousands of animals, domestic and wild, destroyed.

A Personal Account of the Great Fire of 1881

The author's uncle, Gerald F. Thorp was born and raised in the Kingston and Caro area and his lived and worked in the Thumb all his life. He has also long been involved in Masonic organizations in Michigan. In that capacity he has travelled and met with people from all over the state.

In his first job he was a state dairy inspector who travelled the Thumb checking out farms. He has travelled and learned about the area all his life.

When I told him about this book he asked if I would be doing anything on the Great Fires. I said, "of course, you can't understand the Thumb without knowing about the fires." He then told me that in his archives, (that means his desk) he had a second hand account of the fire of 1881. He said I could have it if interested.

Of course I was interested. The story he had was titled, "My Greatest Adventure." It was written by Matlida K. (Ziebell) Gildner, of Grayling, Michigan. Her father Robert Ziebell lived near Port Hope and as a 13 year old boy survived the fire of 1881, and its memory left an indelible mark on him.

He told the story many times, and in 1935, at the age of 67 told the story to his daughter, Matilda. In 1988 someone got her to write her memory of his story, and thank goodness they did. The hair-raising account provides a very clear vision of the fear and horror a young 13 year old felt that hot dry windy day.

Unfortunately Uncle Jerry does not remember how he came in possession of the account.

I was able to trace Matilda Gildner to Grayling where she died in 1998 at the age of 92. This account pulls together many different parts of the story to show how it all played together.

So here is 13 year old Robert Ziebell's account of the Great Fire of 1881 as told to his daughter 55 years later. I kept most typos and grammatical mistakes intact to keep the account as close to the original as possible. I did make a couple of spelling corrections so it would be easier to follow.

It is really interesting to hear Robert talk about the same things that other accounts include, clothes burned off people's back, cattle that couldn't outrun the fire, seeking safety in the lake, people blinded by smoke.

Matilda and her Dad were very good story tellers, read for yourself.

My Greatest Adventure Robert Ziebell

My Greatest adventure is about the fire on the 5th day of September, 1881. I was 13 year old at the time and living at home with my parents in Port Hope, Huron County. The fire swept across three counties, Huron, Sanilac and Tuscola in the State of Michigan.

My father went to Harbor Beach the morning before the

fire with a load of grain with our oxen. Mother and the rest of us were home alone at the time. At about 2 o'clock in the afternoon the wind was blowing so hard. It had been so dry for weeks the farmers were taking advantage of it and clearing the land. In a little while our two neighbors who lived ¼ mile from us (home) burned to the ground, so Mother and the rest of us took our belongings and carried them out on the plowed ground. We took what we could carry and went from the ¼ line (road) to the town line (road) where we would be out of danger. After we were there a few minutes Mother told me she had forgotten the deed of the land (to our family farm) and told me where to get it.

I went back towards our home, I could see black clouds of smoke coming from the west. Those days there was nothing but stumps and log fences. I found the deed and after I found it I couldn't back across the fences, they were all on fire so I had to stay right there and it's a good thing I did. My Father's strawstack was right behind the barn and it caught on fire.

It was leaning and Father had put two big props behind it and when it caught fire I pulled them away, the wind was blowing at such a gale. It picked the straw stack up and it blew into a field where it burned. We had a picket fence in front of our buildings and home.

At about 3:30 in the afternoon, I heard a wagon coming down the road, it turned into our gate. There was Father and the yoke of oxen. I hollered 'Whoa", and the oxen stopped. Father said, "is that you Robert", I said yes, what's the matter Father, he said "help me out, I can't see". Father had long red whiskers, they were burned off his face and his face was all blistered. I helped him out and he asked where Mother and the rest were. I told him where I left them. It worried Father.

It was terrible; you could hear people calling all through the fields, trying to find each other. After the fire kinda died down, Father told me to see if I couldn't find Mother and the children. So I ran about 50 rods, right into a dead woman, everything was burned off of her but her shoes. I stopped right there. I did not go further and believe me if you ever have seen a young Dutchman turn heel, it was me.

The next morning after the fire you could see everything along the road and fields from a chicken to an elephant with the fire started in the wood it chased all the cattle out onto the clearing and when they got to the clearing a farmer had 50 cords of dry hemlock piled along the road and there were the 50 head of cattle burned to death. My Mother and the rest did not return home until the next day. They had been driven to another farmer's place along Lake Huron. Some didn't save a thing, others saved only their bed clothes. The Village of Port Hope did not burn except the saw mill and a few houses. (Author's note, The Port Hope Chimney is all that was left of the mill) There was about 12 that were burned to death around our home that I know of. One family of five children, they found nothing of them but the bones which they buried in a Queen Anne soap box.

The town line where we lived on was at that time 6 or 7 miles long and they were mostly 40 acre farms. On that we had my Father's house, barn and another building. We had six families living with us in our house and barn.

Each family had 3 or 4 children and they lived with us until relief came.

All during the fire there was a partridge that followed me from place to place, but I couldn't get near it. This happened 54 years ago. Many years have passed but this is still a fresh

*memory in my mind. That night when I said my prayers, I
thanked God for his promise of "Always watching over us".*

*This story was told to Robert Ziebell's daughter Matilda
K. Ziebell Gildner Matilda wrote it down January 18, 1988
in 1935.*

Beginnings of the American Red Cross

The catastrophe in the Thumb of Michigan was the first
time the newly founded American Red Cross brought
relief to a disaster area. The American Red Cross did
not take the lead, but did raise $80,000. That was just a
small portion of the relief that was aimed at the Thumb.

Much more money was raised by relief committees
in Detroit and Port Huron, who raised over $800,000
and tons of food and clothing for the survivors of the
Thumb fires.

THUMB NOTE

The International Red Cross began with the
Treaty of Geneva on August 22, 1864. It was
a treaty that dealt with prisoners of war, those
wounded in war, and about disaster relief. Clara
Barton, after working to treat the wounded on both
sides of the American Civil War went to Europe to
work with the new International Red Cross during
the Franco-Prussian War in 1870.

Barton returned home and in March of 1881
she organized the American Red Cross in her
office in Washington D.C. The first Chapter of

the American Red Cross was founded in her home town of Danville, New York on August 22 1881, less than one month before the Thumb disaster. It was the Danville, NY office that issued the first ever Red Cross appeal to help the people of the Thumb.

Senator Omar D. Conger

A side note about the founding of the American Red Cross. Clara Barton was pushing Congress to pass a resolution supporting the Geneva Convention, and founding the American Red Cross.

She met a United States Senator from Michigan, Sen. Omar D. Conger of Port Huron in 1877 and solicited his help. She had Sen. Conger's support because he discovered that she had nursed his brother, Col. Conger, who had been wounded in the Civil War at the battle of Spotsylvania.

Sen. Conger introduced the resolution to support the Geneva Convention and American Red Cross on May 17, 1881. It would be signed the next year by President Chester Arthur.

First elected Judge in St. Clair County in 1848, Senator Omar D. Conger served in the U.S. House of Representative from 1869 till he was appointed U.S. Senator in 1881. He was not re-elected in 1887 and stayed in Washington D.C. to practice law.

After the Catastrophe

The fires of 1881 in the Thumb forever changed the land and people. For 30-40 years after the fires there were few trees in the Thumb. Photos show just how barren the landscape had become.

It's no wonder that much more than a century later you can't understand the Thumb if you don't have some knowledge of the Great Fires.

The fires affected every person who lived in the Thumb. Survivors of the Great Fire of 1881 were sick and blinded by the smoke from the fire. Many couldn't talk or see and had trouble breathing. In some case it was weeks before their health was restored, if then.

The Thumb was still a wilderness in 1881, thankfully lightly populated or the loss of life and property would have been much greater. The loss at the time was estimated at 2.5 million dollars in today's value. A fire of equal intensity today would kill thousands and cost billions.

On September 6, Sgt. William Bailey, from the U. S. Signal Corp. travelled by foot and horse and buggy on an inspection tour. Words from his report are used throughout this story, and some of his descriptions are eerie. He tells of walking over a mile on fallen burned trees through what used to be a forest never touching the ground. He wrote about how you could see nothing for miles except smoldering piles in a devastated forest.

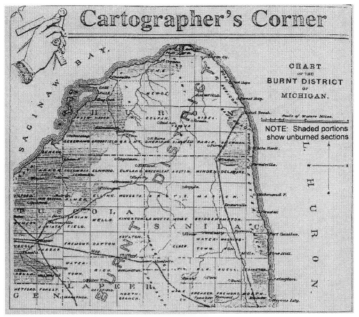

Sgt. Bailey's map of the burned areas

The fire 1881 still impacts every one of us in Michigan today. The fires of 1881 are why today if you want to burn trash on your property you have to check with authorities and get a permit. That is protection for us all. No longer will dozens of farmers be allowed to set fires to clear land on the hottest and driest days of the season.

It is why lumbermen no longer leave slashing in the forest. Today lumbermen own the land and do everything they can to protect their investment. They do not waste a bit of trees harvested from the forests; it is boarded, chopped, stripped and glued for use in a dozen products.

It's hard to imagine but in the aftermath of the fire there was some good news. The fire had cleared away all of the scrub, the slashings and treetops, all the refuse left to rot in the former Thumb wilderness. That was why farmers were starting fires in the first place, to clear their land for agriculture. Now it was all cleared, for those who were left, in one terrible swath.

Final Thoughts on the Great Fires

How did the horror of the fire come about, the loss of life and property the waste; why did it really happen? I'll leave the final word to Rev. E.J. Goodspeed who was responding to those who called it an act of God when he wrote the *History of the Great Fires in Chicago and the West.*

While the good Reverend sounds like he could have written this today, he was actually writing in 1871 when he wrote…

"In our foolish American Haste we have wastefully cut down the trees, dried up the springs, raised the temperature so that precipitation of moisture is reduced, and have driven the rain away in useless clouds of invisible vapor over the Atlantic. We have prayed for rain one day of the week and driven it away with an axe on six. Now whose fault was it? We (I am) are not inclined to shift the blame to heaven. It is we who have created these dry summers. Men, not provider, brought this calamity on us."

Blue Water Highway

Our Thumb Drive will generally follow a beautiful road around Michigan's Thumb. It was originally called US 25, and today is M-25. For most of the trip you will drive right along Saginaw Bay and Lake Huron.

According to Dr. LeRoy Barnett in his book *A Drive Down Memory Lane: The named State and Federal Highways in Michigan* it all started with the opening of the Blue Water Bridge in Port Huron in 1938. No longer would travelers have to wait for slow ferries, they could breeze across the border and St. Clair River on the Bridge.

But while the bridge was hurrying up travel, the roads into Michigan were problematic. M-25 around the Thumb had 40 miles of dirt road bed. In December of 1938, 300 Thumb residents met in Harbor Beach to discuss the road and what they could do to improve it. They created the "Michigan Blue Water Highway Association", and from that name they named the road the "Blue Water Highway", a great name and description of the road.

So here we go; a trip on the Blue Water Highway, along Saginaw Bay and Lake Huron, through history and small towns.

We will meet and learn about people who have touched the Thumb. Some of the place names we will find on our journey, Wisner, Sleeper and White Rock for example will give us an opportunity to learn more about Michigan.

Thumb Places

As we begin our Thumb tour we start on M-83. We'll start in one of my favorite places in the state, one of the most popular tourist attractions in the nation, Frankenmuth.

Chapter 3

Franken Thumbs to Gera

Franken Thumbs *(hilf-muth-lust-trost)*

Frankenmuth was settled in 1845 by Lutheran immigrants from Franconia, now part of Bavaria, in Germany. The Franken part of the name represents the part of Germany most of the immigrants came from, Franconia in the Kingdom of Bavaria. The "mut" part of the name means courage. The courage of the Franconians is celebrated because of the fortitude they showed when they left their homes to go to a new land. Today over half of the people who live in Frankenmuth are of German descent.

They came to form a mission to minister to the Indians and to "Lutheranize" them. They bought 680 acres of an Indian reservation for their town. Unfortunately there was a problem; the Indians were already leaving the area, looking for better hunting grounds than the cleared areas of the "white man's" farms.

Today, the City of Frankenmuth is famous for its Bavarian theme and chicken dinners. They have been served in Frankenmuth since the 1920s. But how did the Bavarian theme happen?

While it is true that a great number of residents are of German extraction, that is not the whole reason. The reason for the Bavarian theme: Interstate 75 was built seven miles away. Before the only way north was M-83, the main street through Frankenmuth. That is why they had road houses that served chicken dinners. But when President Eisenhower began to build the interstate in the 1950s some places were left behind, one of the places bypassed was Frankenmuth.

The story goes the William "Tiny" Zehnder visited the old country, Germany's Franconia or Bavaria region. He got this idea of recreating the culture and look of Bavaria in his little town of Frankenmuth. It was the only way to attract visitors to drive that long seven miles to their town.

To say it worked would be an understatement. Today you can stop for; a famous chicken dinner at the Bavarian Inn or Zehnders across the street, see the world's largest Christmas store, Bronner's, enjoy the Bavarian Festival or Johnny Burke's Chicken and Lobster Fest, go for a drive across the covered bridge, a ride on a paddlewheel boat on the Cass River, or to visit brew pubs and Wineries. Frankenmuth is one of the top tourist attractions anywhere in the country.

Germans continued to come to the area from Franconia even after they no longer served as mission post for the spread of Christianity to the Chippewa tribe. It was about the farm land, good earth, and the fact they could go to a place where their German language would be understood.

Continuing north on M-83 we'll see three small villages.

FRANKENTROST, founded in 1847, the "trost", or as it was first called Trostville, being German for comfort or consolation.

FRANKENLUST founded in 1848. The "lust" in their name is German for pleasure.

FRANKENHILF founded in 1851. The "hilf" was German for assistance. Actually you won't see Frankenhilf anymore; the name was changed in 1862 to Richville. The story of how Richville got its name is interesting. It was said the conductors on trains through Frankenmuth and into the Thumb couldn't pronounce the name Frankenhilf, so they just started calling it Richville, for the rich farm land around it.

From the collection of Alan Loftis

Gera

A bit further north on M-83 into the Thumb you come to road crossing that used to be a stop on the Central Railroad called "Frankenmuth Station." In 1878 the Port Huron & North Western started building a railroad into Michigan's thumb and by 1882, it reached Gera. It later became part of the Flint & Pere Marquette Railroad. The Pere Marquette was taken over by the C&O, which in turn became part of CSX.

Businessmen in Frankenmuth didn't want to give the railroad a right of way, so they built the depot just 3 miles north in Gera. The building was built in Vassar for a pumper employee, to pump water into steam locomotives. It was loaded on a flat car and moved to Gera.

Frankenmuth Station was renamed Gera in 1894 for a City in Germany.

There is no longer a train station in Gera, but the old depot is still in the area. It was moved to a local backyard where you might see it as you drive by today.

You continue on north on M-83 through beautiful, flat farm country with large farms and huge barns. When you get to Bay City M-83 ends at M-25, the Blue Water Highway. We will turn right, or east to travel the tip of the Thumb. But first a few words on Bay City.

Chapter 4

To the Bay

Bay City

Bay City was founded in 1831 as a trading post built by brothers named Trombley.

In 1836 the Village of Lower Saginaw was platted. There was a Post Office that took the name Hampton after the Township. In 1846 it was renamed Lower Saginaw.

But according to stories the residents didn't like name "Lower Saginaw" so in 1857 they renamed it Bay City

If you had gone west, or left, on M-25, actually it would have been Center Street, you would see a large number of mansions along the street. These were the homes of people who made fortunes in the Lumbering, and shipbuilding business. These are the industries that built the town and many fortunes.

Until 1905, the City of Bay City was only on the east bank of the Saginaw River, the west bank was a separate city known as West Bay City.

Actually West Bay City was first known as Lake City, but there was already a Lake City in Michigan so they renamed it Wenona, after the mother of Hiawatha in the poem by Henry Wadsworth Longfellow.

Wenona Park, an amusement park, began in the 1870s and closed in 1964, after 90 years. It had a casino, rides, trains, swim beaches, and lots of food. Today, a trailer park occupies this land along the shores of the Saginaw Bay.

Wenona incorporated as a village in 1867, and, 10 years later the Michigan Legislature consolidated Wenona with two other nearby villages, Banks and Salzburgh to form the city of West Bay City. Finally in 1905, West Bay City merged with Bay City.

Jane (Johnston) Schoolcraft

THUMB NOTE

If you remember earlier I talked about Henry Schoolcraft who made up names that sounded like Indian names for counties all over Michigan. He also wrote a book describing the stories his wife, the Granddaughter of an Ojibwa Chief had told him.

Jane (Johnston) Schoolcraft was the granddaughter of Ojibwa Chief Waubojeeg.

She and her husband wrote stories based on her knowledge of the Ojibwa legends she learned as a girl with her husband. Henry Wadsworth Longfellow read the book and used the stories in his epic "Song of Hiawatha."

Longfellow describes Wenona…

"There among the ferns and mosses,
There among the prairie lilies,
In the moonlight and the starlight,
Fair Nokomis bore a daughter.
And she called her name Wenonah,
As the first-born of her daughters.
And the daughter of Nokomis

Grew up like the prairie lilies,
Grew a tall and slender maiden,
With the beauty of the moonlight,
With the beauty of the starlight."

In the story Nokomis warns Wenona about Mudjekeewis the bear, who, in Ojibwa myth, is a spirit, and figures prominently in their storytelling, including their story of the world's creation.

In The Song of Hiawatha Mudjekeewis, the bear, ravishes Wenonah and fathers Hiawatha. Here is the opening of Longfellow's epic.

"Song of Hiawatha."

By the shores of Gitche Gumee,
By the shining Big-Sea-Water,
Stood the wigwam of Nokomis,
Daughter of the Moon, Nokomis.
Dark behind it rose the forest,
Rose the black and gloomy pine-trees,
Rose the firs with cones upon them;
Bright before it beat the water,
Beat the clear and sunny water,
Beat the shining Big-Sea-Water.
There the wrinkled old Nokomis
Nursed the little Hiawatha,
Rocked him in his linden cradle,
Bedded soft in moss and rushes,
Safely bound with reindeer sinews;
Stilled his fretful wail by saying,
"Hush! the Naked Bear will hear thee!"

Hampton Township

Hampton was what the Bay City area was first called. The Dutch came to the area in 1855 and set about using the rich flat land for farming. The Dutch were the perfect people to settle this area as it was swampy and full of stumps left over from the lumbering era.

In their native home, The Netherlands, the people had to drain swamps and steal land from the ocean to survive. So when they arrived in the Thumb the Dutch knew how to build drainage canals to keep the land dry for farming. Some of those drains look like small rivers. Actually, many rivers aren't that big. As you travel through you can't miss these drains running in fields and along roads. It can be intimidating to drive down a road with an open drain that is larger than the road running alongside.

The farms in Hampton Township grow potatoes, sugar beets, corn and beans on their reclaimed swamp land.

Quanicassee

Quanicassee is really what's left of a small settlement along Saginaw Bay in Tuscola County. The name is of Native American origin, it means "lone tree". It had a post office with the name "Quanicasse City" from 1886-1902.

The place has been settled for so long that there are no clear records as to who was the first European to settle there.

The area was an Indian fishing village long before the arrival of white settlers, and it still is a great place to wet a line, and put your boat in the water for a day on the Bay.

Wisner

Quanicasse is in Wisner Township, which also includes the crossroads community of Wisner. The first to take land in this area were; Joshua Terry, who came in 1853, Green Bird who arrived in 1854 and Isaiah Jester in 1855.

Governor Moses Wisner

They began to organize the township in 1861 and named it for Moses Wisner, who was just then completing his only term as Governor of Michigan. He served from 1859–1861.

THUMB NOTE

Moses Wisner was the twelfth Governor of Michigan. He was born in Springport, New York on June 3, 1815. In 1837, he moved to Michigan and settled in Lapeer County, where he worked as a farmer and studied law.

He was admitted to the bar in 1841, and then began his legal career. He would practice law and serve as the Lapeer County prosecuting attorney.

In 1862, the year after he left office, he organized the 22nd Michigan Infantry and was commissioned colonel. In one of the tragic stories of the war he never made it to the battlefield. In

1863, on the way to join his troops, Governor Wisner contracted typhoid fever and died in Kentucky at age 47.

Judge Charles Wisner

But the Wisner story doesn't end there. His son, Judge Charles Wisner, known as "Chip" became famous in Flint as part of its automotive heritage. It was Judge Wisner who built the first automobile ever built in the Vehicle City. He called that vehicle his "Buzz Wagon" because it made such a racket that it frightened his horses and neighbors in the Court Street, Lapeer Street area near downtown Flint. Judge Wisner had other problems with his famous "Buzz Wagon" besides the noise, like its lack of brakes. That made for a unique way of stopping his machine. He had to run into the side of a building, usually his carriage barn, to stop it. Maybe that's why even though he built 3 models of the contraption none were ever manufactured.

Governor Wisner's son, Judge Charles "Chip" Wisner died in 1915 at age 65 after 21 years as a judge.

You can still see Judge Wisner's carriage barn, which is what we call a garage today. It was saved from the wrecking ball during the construction of I-475 through Flint in 1973 by being moved to the Genesee County Parks-Crossroads Village; an 1890s village made up of historic buildings that were brought there to save for the future.

Unionville

In 1853 Private Marvin W. Kramer was given the land in the area for his service in the War of 1812. He called it Kramertown; a name that didn't last very long, neither did Mr. Kramer who seems to have disappeared.

Horace Marvin arrived in about 1854 from Union, Ohio and built the first log cabin home in town. He named it after his home town, later it became Unionville. Unionville became incorporated as village on April 1, 1853, with Mr. Marvin becoming the first village president. Its first post office opened in 1858, with Samuel B. Covey as its postmaster.

Most of the early settlers were farmers, but lumbering was also an important way to make a living.

It paid more money, it was not as much of a gamble as farming and there were lots of trees. Lumbering was the first big industry in the area. But after the forests were lumbered, and the great fires of 1871 and 1881, lumbering ended and once again farming took over as the major industry of the area.

According to the Unionville Website, the first village ordinances included "livestock prohibited from running at large, no fire crackers and baseball playing was prohibited on business streets."

Chapter 5

Thumbs West Shore

Sebewaing

Sebewaing is in Huron County and is situated right on Saginaw Bay. The town's name came from the native American Ojibwa word meaning, "crooked creek", or, "by the stream."

In the 1860's migrants began to arrive from Germany to join those who had already settled in places like Frankenmuth and Frankentrost. Like in those communities it was a Lutheran Minister from Ann Arbor who first came, for the good farmland, but mostly to do mission work with the Indians.

Like all good German communities Sebewaing needed a brewery.

In 1880 the E.O. Braendle Brewery began operations, by 1927 it was renamed, the Sebewaing Brewing Company.

They brewed many German-style beers in the town until it closed in 1966. You can still find Sebewaing Beer at the Michigan Brewing company in Webberville, Michigan. Using authentic recipes and labels they have resurrected some of the brands.

THUMB NOTE

Here's an interesting note; a relative of a former brewery worker said that on the last day of the Sebewaing Brewing Company, June 4, 1966, a number of unused beer cans were run through the canning equipment, and filled with air. The idea was to use the cans as "fishing net floats". You can still find some of those air filled cans on the internet for sale.

Today the Thumb is noted for its huge crops of sugar beets. Michigan Sugar has a large presence in many Thumb communities, including Sebewaing. That is why it is known as the Sugar Capital of Michigan.

The annual Michigan Sugar Festival is one of the community's signature events and a great place to visit in the middle of June. The purpose of the festival is "To show the area's appreciation to the sugar industry which has purchased sugar beet crops from farmers and processed sugar here with local employees since 1902." The first Sugar Festival was in 1965, and continues strong to this day.

BayPort

Bay Port is now and always has been a fishing port. It is located off of Wildfowl Bay, on the Westside of Michigan's Thumb. It was first called Geneva by one of its first settlers, Carl Heisterman, who arrived in around 1851. He later changed it to Switzerland, then to Wildfowl Port, finally Bay Port in 1872. Mr. Heisterman's name is memorialized on Heisterman Island, just offshore in the Bay!

In 1880, Jesse Hoyt of New York began the Saginaw, Tuscola and Huron Railroad. It brought tourists to Bay Port from East Saginaw for rock hunting excursions at the Bay Port Quarry. Rocks and stone slabs are still an important business after more than a century. They continue to be mined and sold in Bay Port.

In 1886 a 117 room first class hotel was built on Cedar St and Second St, the steps still remain at the site. It had a casino, billiards, bowling, & electric lights.

Later the hotel became the Bay Port Club. It was torn down in 1907 because tourists were no longer as interested in rocks at the quarry as they had been, and the water receded so the hotel was farther away from the Bay.

If you like fish, and fish sandwiches, then the place to be in the first full weekend in August is Bay Port's Fish Sandwich Festival. That's when thousands of visitors eat tens of thousands of fish sandwiches.

Chapter 6

Cheeseburgers, Perch and Ports

Caseville

Continuing up the Blue Water Highway you come to one of the Thumbs hottest communities, Caseville, sometimes referred to as the, "Perch Capital" of Michigan. It is located at the mouth of the Pigeon River on Saginaw Bay and has been a vacation spot and travel destination in Michigan for decades.

Beautiful beaches, great fishing and second growth forests line M-25, Caseville's main street. It has a great view of Saginaw Bay, and freighters that sail past. There are many restaurants, camping and a charming downtown shopping area. Caseville is a Harbor of Refuge with boating and launch facilities that beckon anglers in search of walleye, perch, trout and more.

It was first settled in 1836 by a man named Ruben Dodge as Pigeon River Settlement, and sometimes even called, "The Mouth." It was first a lumbering area and then became known for ship building and even salt mining.

In 1852 William Rattle representing Leonard Case of Cleveland, who owned all the land in the area, put up a saw mill. At this time, he renamed the town Port Elizabeth, or Elizabeth Town, after his wife.

In 1856 Francis Crawford bought 20,000 acres from Case to found a village. Mr. Case was certainly swayed by the fact that Crawford would call his new town, Caseville.

In 1999, a summer festival was founded in Caseville based on pop singer/songwriter Jimmy Buffett's song, "Cheeseburger in Paradise." That summer the festival brought in about 5,000 people. Today the Cheeseburger in Caseville Festival is a 10 day event, at the end of August that attracts upwards of 50,000 people with concerts, fireworks, and, the highlight of the festival, The Parade of Tropical Fools-held on the first Wednesday night of the festival and is the biggest attraction that the festival has to offer.

Sleeper State Park

Continuing down M-25, just east of Caseville, you'll find one of the oldest state parks in Michigan, Sleeper State Park. Sleeper is 723 acres of forest, wetlands, sandy beach and dunes located on the Saginaw Bay.

You can dip your feet into the lake, get sand between your toes, take hikes on many trails and see both a Michigan sunrise and sunset at this unique location.

The park first opened as a county park in 1925. In 1927 the state obtained the property and called it Huron State Park. In 1944, the park was renamed in honor of Albert E. Sleeper, Governor of Michigan and a resident of Huron County. It was Governor Sleeper, who signed the law that created the state park system.

THUMB NOTE

Albert Edson Sleeper was the 29th Governor of Michigan, serving two terms from1917 to 1921. He actually grew up in Bradford, Vermont where he was born in 1862. When he was 22 he moved to Lexington, Michigan where he became a very successful businessman owning several banks and much real estate. He served as a State Senator and as the State Treasurer before being elected Governor in 1916.

Governor Albert Sleeper

Besides being the Michigan Governor who created the state parks system, he also was in office when; the Department of Labor was formed, the first Public Utilities Commission was created, he started the county roads system and initiated the Michigan State Troops Permanent Force, which became the Michigan State Police It was during his terms that the first Michigan Driver's License was issued.

Governor Sleeper died in Lexington on May 13, 1934 at the age of seventy-one and is buried at Lexington Municipal Cemetery.

Pinnebog originally Pinne Pog

Pinnebog is one of my two favorite place names in the Thumb, along with Quanicassee. Pinnebog was such a popular name that two communities fought over it. The Pinnebog along the Blue Water Highway isn't there anymore. The Pinnebog that exists today is a bit inland, south of M-25 on the Kinde Road. The Pinnebog along the lake shore is now called Port Crescent, which is a ghost town and a state park, more on that coming up.

The inland Pinnepog first changed its name to

Pinnebog to refer to the "Pine Bog" in the area, and to differentiate it from the Pinnepog on the shore of the Bay, along what is now M-25.

But there was still confusion so Pinnepog changed its name to Port Crescent.

The township in which Pinnebog exists, Hume Township, is in Huron County and is named after the first white settler in the area. Walter Hume, who arrived and built the first house in the 1850s, built a hotel at the mouth of the Pinnebog River That might have been the first commercial building in the area. The Township was organized in 1860, at Hume's store, the first election was held at Hume's Store and Mr. Hume was elected the first supervisor.

The land had once been covered with pine trees, but they had mostly been felled and sent to sawmills at Port Crescent on the mouth of the Pinnebog River long ago. The fires of 1871 and 1881 destroyed most of what was left of the timber land.

THUMB NOTE

Port Crescent State Park is the site of the original Pinnepog. It includes 3 miles of Lake Huron beachfront, sand dunes, dune forest, and backwaters and bayous of the Pinnebog River. The site was once the prosperous logging and sand-mining town of Port Crescent. Henry Ford of the Ford Motor Company built a huge sand mining and shipping operation in the area. There are still some reminders of the areas' industrial past. The town and most of the mining remains have long since disappeared; reclaimed by nature.

Today Port Crescent State park is one of the few places you'll find sand dunes in the eastern part of Michigan. The park is a major birding area. From March through April, broad-winged hawks and other birds-of-prey congregate here before continuing their journey to northern breeding grounds. You can also see Loons, bluebirds, Wild turkeys and blue herons.

Port Austin

Port Austin is right at the tip of the Thumb, a beautiful place to look out over Lake Huron and enjoy the cool lake breeze. It is one of the few places in the world where you can watch both a sunrise and sunset.

How Port Austin became Port Austin is a great story in itself. In about 1839 a settler and sawmill owner named Jonathon Byrd came to the area. He called the settlement Byrd's Creek and settled along a creek that is still called Byrd's Creek. He sold his interest to the Smith, Austin & Dwight, Lumber firm, and they renamed the community Dwight.

Later Mr. P.C. Austin, part owner in that lumber firm, and owner of a sawmill, built a boat dock for himself. It worked so well for him he saw a business opportunity and enlarged it so he could get others to use his dock. That's when the place became known as Austin's Dock.

He then realized that his dock couldn't be seen in the evening or at night, so he put a street light on a pole on his dock and called it a "lighthouse." At that point it became known as Austin's Light, later as Austin's Port, and finally as Port Austin.

For a time the east side of the town continued to be called Dwight, but they finally compromised. The Post Office Department said they had to pick one name or the other or they couldn't have a post office. So, the entire village became Port Austin, and the Township was named Dwight.

Port Austin Reef Light

THUMB NOTE

One of the most visible historic sites around Port Austin, the Port Austin Reef Light was authorized by Congress in 1856 to cost $82,151.14. The lighthouse is at the juncture of Saginaw Bay and Lake Huron. It is the "turning point" for both northbound shipping and westbound shipping as they turn into Saginaw Bay. You can see it from the mainland and the docks in downtown Port Austin.

The original light was finally built in 1878 to warn ships of the long dangerous shoal or reef that runs just under the lake at the tip of the Thumb. The house was abandoned by its keepers in 1953, when they were able to pull an underwater cable to the site to power the light, which is 2.5 miles from Port Austin, about 1.5 miles from other points on the mainland. The house was left to rapidly deteriorate.

The Port Austin Reef Light Association got a lease to work on restoration of the buildings at the light. Their first big battle was to oust the at least 500 pigeons, and the refuse they left for half a century. The building was reroofed, bird proofed, and reclaimed for mankind. Interior renovation began in 1990.

In June 2011, the Port Austin Light, along with 11 other lighthouses, was made available at no cost to groups willing to preserve them. On July 19, 2012 the Port Austin Reef Lighthouse Association, a Michigan non-profit organization, took ownership of the Port Austin Light Station to continue their work.

The light is not open for tours; it is a long and difficult trip to the light, which is always hindered by the reef, and often by the fog. However, it is possible to photograph the lighthouse from shore.

Chapter 7

The "T" At the Tip of the Thumb

The Heart of the Thumb

As you get to the center of Port Austin, on M-25, you come to a light. Off to the left is Lake Huron, the State of Michigan Harbor and docks, and out past the docks and break wall, out about 2.5 miles, is the Port Austin Reef Light.

Turning right you continue on M-25, but at this point it is also M-53. M-25 continues for a mile or so and passes the Garfield Inn and the 1884 Bank, as you'll read in a moment, and then turns to the east or left. But if you were to continue south on M-53 it would take you to Bad Axe, one of the Thumb's biggest communities, and to Cass City, named for Lewis Cass.

Let's take some time to cross the T of the Thumb with a quick trip down M-53.

Bad Axe

According to legend the eye catching name, Bad Axe, came about in 1861. Rudolph Papst and George Willis Pack were surveying a state road (today's M-53) through the Huron County wilderness when they decided to make camp in an abandoned hunter's shack they came across. In that shack they found an old and rusty axe. To identify the place in their survey they used the name "bad axe camp" on their map. And that is how Bad Axe first appeared on a Michigan map.

Bad Axe was incorporated as a village in 1885 and became Huron County's first city on March 15, 1905.

Cass City

Cass City as well as the Cass River are named for Governor Lewis Cass, one of the most influential and important people in Michigan history.

Lewis Cass

THUMB NOTE

Born in Exeter, New Hampshire in October of 1782, Lewis Cass moved to Marietta, Ohio in 1800. Cass was a founder of the Grand Masonic Lodge of Ohio, and later co-founded the Grand Lodge of Michigan as well, being elected as its first Grand Master.

Among his many accomplishments, he negotiated treaties with Indian tribes, was appointed Territorial Governor of Michigan and served for 18 years (1813-1831) as a reward for his service as a Brigadier General in the war of 1812. He served as; an American Ambassador to France, Secretary of War under President Andrew Jackson, Secretary of State under President James Buchanan, a U.S. Senator representing Michigan and a two time losing candidate for President of the United States.

Cass died in 1866 and is buried in Elmwood Cemetery in Detroit, Michigan.

Among the famous people who were born in Cass City are Baseball Hall of Famer "Larry"

Leland Stanford MacPhail, Sr., and Astronaut Brewster Saw.

Larry MacPhail's father was a banker who owned many small banks around the state. Larry went to the University of Michigan and attended Law School at George Washington University Law School where he met baseball innovator Branch Rickey. In 1933 he was hired by the Cincinnati Reds as general manager. He went on to serve as president/general manager of the Brooklyn Dodgers and the New York Yankees. Among MacPhail's innovations; nighttime baseball, regular game televising and the flying of teams between games.

MacPhail was elected to the Baseball Hall of Fame in 1978; his son Lee MacPhail also a baseball man and President of the American League was elected to the Hall in 1998, making them the only father and son inductees. Larry MacPhail died in 1975 and is buried at Elkland Township Cemetery in Cass City

Brewster Shaw, Jr. grew up in Michigan and graduated from Cass City High School in 1963. He is a former NASA astronaut, a retired U.S. Air Force colonel and former executive at Boeing.

Shaw flew three space shuttle missions and has logged 533 hours of space flight. He was pilot of space shuttle Columbia in November 1983, commander of space shuttle Atlantis in November 1985 and commander of Columbia in August 1989. Shaw was inducted into the U.S. Astronaut Hall of Fame in 2006.

Huron Petroglyphs-Sanilac Petroglyphs

Ancient Michigan natives carved swirls and stick figures that lasted thousands of years covered by the Thumb forest, till the Great Fires cleared it away. Photo by Steven Hester.

Also down M-53 you'll find the only ancient rock art yet discovered in Michigan.

The carvings include; swirls, lines, handprints, flying birds and bow-wielding men, left by Native American Indians in the region at the Sanilac Petroglyphs Historic State Park.

The carvings, as mentioned in the chapter about the Great Fires of 1881, were discovered by residents after the fire swept through the area and burned off the growth and uncovered rocks bearing the designs.

Geologists say the carvings were made 300 to 1,000 years ago, dating back to the Late Woodland Period. The sandstone where the petroglyphs were carved is a soft stone that allowed Native Americans to cut it easily. Sadly the soft stone also has allowed weather and more modern graffiti artists to add their scrawls and destroy the ancient doodles. That is why today the area is fenced in and protected from the elements as well as modern taggers.

Thumb Octagon Barn

Down M-53, near Gagetown, you'll find one of the largest barns you'll ever see. The ground floor of the barn measures 8,600 square feet and the loft area 5,700 square feet for a combined total of 14,300 square feet...now that's a barn!

The story begins 1869 when James Luther Purdy was born in Pontiac, Michigan. By 1890 he joined his father at the Bank of P.C. Purdy and Son in Gagetown.

He married Cora Ozella Warner of Cass City in 1894 and they lived above the bank in Gagetown.

The Purdy Bank was quite successful and was one of two banks in Michigan to remain solvent during the Great Depression. Mr. Purdy was one of the Michigan bankers who pushed to get the Federal Government to insure the investor's money in banks. He traveled to Washington to talk to Michigan Republican Senator Arthur Vandenberg (Grand Rapids) who introduced the bill into the Senate. President Franklin Roosevelt also supported the idea and that led to the formation of the Federal Deposit Insurance Corporation (the FDIC).

Meanwhile, in his travels Purdy saw an octagonal barn and decided he wanted one too. In 1895 he bought a 40 acre parcel of land just east of Richie Road, and later 520 acres more to build his new barn.

Local Craftsman George and John Munro were hired in 1923 to build the barn. They had already built Purdy's 15-room house in 1919. The Munro's consulted with Russell Jaggers, Principal and mathematics teacher at Gagetown High School, to help with the mathematical calculations necessary to construct an octagonal building. To the tip of the weathervane the barn is 70 ft. tall and covers approximately 3/16 of an acre and it contains hundreds of windows, which are set so, it seems, the sun would not directly hit the hay stored in the loft.

It has a rail system in the upper floors to move the hay and had scales, a tack room, a dairy and much more. What do you expect with an octagon barn that includes over 14 thousand square feet.

After his brother George died John Munro moved to Albion, Michigan where he continued building homes. The most well-known is Bellemont Manor, at Albion College which is used today as its Continuing Education Center. It was originally built for George Dean, President of Union Steel Products.

You can visit the Thumb Octagon Barn; thanks to the Friends of the Thumb Octagon Barn organization who saved this unique treasure from the wrecking ball and have added much more to the site. Be sure you stop for a visit.

Thumb More

You can't visit the Thumb of Michigan without checking out what happens in the middle of the digit. We've traveled around the Blue Water Highway, M-25, and taken a quick trip south to see Bad Axe, Unionville and Cass City, but what about Caro, Vassar, Kingston and Wahjamega; those places more central in the Thumb.

Let's head west on M-81 toward Caro, the center of the Thumb.

Caro

Caro was first known as Centerville. Let me start by saying that Caro is a special place for me. First, along with Kingston, it is where the Thorp family is from, so I spent a lot of weekends and summers on the farm in Wells Township on Bevens Road. It was also the place where I got my first full time job in radio, at WKYO. The studios were located in the old city hall, in the center of downtown, next to Thurb's Barber Shop on State Road right across from the old Montague Hotel.

WKYO 1360 AM

I started at AM 1360 in 1973, working weekends. WKYO was licensed as a daytime Station by the FCC. That means it was on from sunrise till sunset every day. I first worked on Saturday's from noon till sunset, whenever that was, and on Sunday from sunrise till sunset! Sunrise was set at 5:30, no matter the time of actual sunrise, but it was later as the days got longer. So, on a Sunday I might work from 5:30AM till 5:45PM, (in December), or all the way until 9:45 PM, (in July). That made for some pretty long days, but that was OK by me; because I wanted to be on the radio!

Mine was also the first voice ever heard on WKYO FM, today it is WIDL FM.

When they were doing transmitter tests I recorded a tape that ran on a loop for several days, "You're listening to WKYO FM, Caro, conducting studio transmitter tests."

I did newscasts, played music of all kinds, travelled all over the Thumb learning to do football and basketball play by play live on the air, did the WKYO Pooch Parade, ("News of animals lost and found, and pets to give away." Some things you never forget.), and hosted the WKYO Morning Farm Report. Now that was quite a feat for a city kid from the north end of Flint. I learned my business in Caro, and met many characters.

Meeting Thumb Characters

It was easy for me to get to meet these characters since I worked on the radio and my family was from there.

Through an uncle I met the late Dorr Wiltse a local teacher then insurance agent in Caro. Dorr Wiltse was a storyteller and historian who collected stories of his home town and wrote a book about it in 1983. I've had it for years and read it many times. He told some great stories in his book, A look In Your Own Back Yard or Tales of Caro and Nearby Places. I admit freely that I found many stories in his book. It is thanks to Dorr Wiltse that many of these stories have been saved.

The first European to see the Cass River and the Caro area may well have been the French writer Alexis de Tocqueville the author of Democracy in America.

The story of de Tocqueville in Michigan is fun to tell. He came to the new world in 1831 to 'see the wilderness." The story goes that when he got to Detroit, which was a backwater place then, he asked where the wilderness was. The residents told him this was it. He wanted to get to the real wilderness so he asked, "Where should I not go"? The people said he should not go to Saginaw, there was nothing there. So, of course that is where he went.

THUMB NOTE

He wrote about his visit in Democracy in America. He went through Flint and wrote the story of tavern keeper John Todd's watch bear. A black bear chained to the front of his tavern to act as a sort of watch dog/bear. He talked about getting to the mouth of the Saginaw River. When Tocqueville returned south down the Saginaw he went down the Cass River, likely to where the present day City of Caro is located today.

De Tocqueville was able to illustrate the places he saw, and the American people in a way that accurately describes us and predicts the future in many ways. Here is a great example of one of his visionary passages in *Democracy in America*.

"In a few years these impenetrable forests will have fallen.

The sons of civilization will break the silence of the Saginaw.

The banks will be imprisoned with quays: it's current which now flows on unnoticed

And tranquil through a nameless waste, will

Be stemmed by the prows of vessels. We were perhaps the last

travelers allowed to see the primitive grandeur of the solitude."

He might well have been the last to see the Thumb as wilderness!

The first settlers in the area were; Ebenezer Davis who is said to be the first permanent white settler in Tuscola County, arriving in 1835, and William F. Sherman who got to Caro in 1850 looking for lumber.

William Sherman, born in Oakland County in 1829, is a key figure in everything that happened in Caro for many years. He even gave the place its names, both of them. He liked the area so much he convinced his father, Samuel, who had been living in Oakland County, to build a house there, the first house in the town, and it still exists. Interestingly, it was the home of Dorr Wiltse for many years.

In 1856 the State of Michigan decided they needed a road from Bridgeport to Forestville on Lake Huron in Sanilac County. That brought a number of people to town to build a road. Builders, and visitors, need a place to stay so a man named Melvin Gibbs came to town to open a hotel to board the workers in a log building owned by Samuel Sherman. That building also still exists in Caro.

The next year William Sherman decided that a hotel was not a bad idea and opened his own. He named his hotel the Centerville House, because it was at the center of the Thumb. The residents at the time liked the name, and since they had not named their little community it became known as Centerville. This was the first time William Sherman named his town, but not the last.

It was also William Sherman who gave the town its new and current name, Caro. In 1868 the town was still known as Centerville when they asked the federal government for a post office.

The state of Michigan already had a Centerville. That village was actually spelled Centreville and is the county seat of St. Joseph County. So, they had to come up with another name quick.

Mr. Sherman, as the story goes, was a big fan of Cairo, Egypt. According to legend, and Dorr Wiltse, he wrote down Caro. No one knows if he was a bad speller or left the "i" out intentionally, but we do know that in 1869 the legislature of Michigan approved the name. It may be the only place in the world named Caro.

Samuel Sherman purchased a lot of land in the area, so his children joined him. His daughters married and they and their new husbands joined them as well. One daughter married a man named Gamble, the other a man named MacPhail. Both built on Mr. Sherman's property.

William MacPhail was probably born in Scotland in around 1827. He married Isabelle Sherman, daughter of Samuel and they had a son named Curtis born in 1857. Curtis graduated in 1875 from Caro High School and became a banker. He moved to Cass City where he married and had a son, Leland Stanford MacPhail, born in 1890.

Why is the MacPhail family important to our story of the Thumb?

Leland was better known as Larry, he was a graduate of the University of Michigan law School, an attorney and a baseball executive. You've already learned about him, and his son, Lee from our story about Cass City.

Another famous name that got its start in the Thumb was George Getty. George was another graduate of the University of Michigan Law School. Attorney Getty came to Caro in 1882, immediately after passing the bar exam. He married a woman from Caro, Sarah McKenney, the daughter of a local pastor.

George F. Getty made a lot of investments that did well for him, and he began to do some research on a new and booming industry, petroleum. In about 1890 he and Sarah moved to Duluth, Minnesota, so he could take a job as an attorney for oil interests there. He invested in that industry and did pretty well again.

By 1892 George and Sarah had moved to Minneapolis and welcomed a son, Jean Paul. He learned the new oil business from his father, who started in the oil business in Caro. Getty got into the industry and made some pretty good investments himself. By the time J. Paul Getty died in 1976 he was one of the richest men on earth, a fortune that began in a law office in Caro, Michigan.

There were some well-known retailers that got their start in Caro as well.

In the 1870's three brothers came to town, directly from Bay City, but indirectly from Riga, Russia. They were what were known as "pack peddlers." They would pack goods and carry them around and sell them. The First brother, Wolf Himmelhoch got to Bay City in 1873; he packed his way to Caro and decided to stay. He sent for his brothers Meyer and Isaac. Together they worked and did very well. In the 1890's they opened a store in Caro.

In 1907 Wolf decided that Detroit was going to boom, so he moved there and opened Himmelhoch's on Woodward Avenue. It was said that Himmelhoch's was second only to Hudson's as a department Store; and it all started in Caro.

Another set of brothers, Joseph, Solomon and Abraham, came to America and got their start in Caro. They were all born in Syria in the 1880's and came to America in1900. When they got to Cleveland they heard about jobs in the sugar beet fields of Tuscola County.

First they worked the fields, and at the sugar factory, then they decided to try something new these, "Hamady Brothers" would sell fresh produce in a shop they opened a store on main street. By 1907 they were on their way. In 1920 the Hamadys wanted to expand, so they closed up that shop and moved to Flint where "Hamady Brothers Food Markets" became an icon.

There were two newspapers in Caro for some years; the Tuscola County Advertiser which still is published and the Tuscola County Courier. The Courier was published by Grant Slocum. He was a writer, thinker and businessman. He published "The Gleaner Monthly", which was a big agricultural newspaper and the official publication of the Ancient Order of Gleaners, a fraternal organization and an insurance organization. It outgrew its Caro office and in 1909 moved to Detroit. The organization still is in operation today.

Grant's son, George was a graduate of the Caro High School Class of 1906, and when his Dad went to Detroit, he went too. He was also a writer and publisher. In 1925 he founded and published "The Automotive Journal." Later it became the "Automotive News' and remains part of Crain's Communications in Detroit.

Sugar beets are big business in the Thumb. As anyone knows during harvest you can get stuck behind trucks and wagons loaded with beets. There are mountains of beets at sugar factories around the Thumb. In 1899 Peninsular Sugar completed its factory in Caro, and it continued to grow for years. It became the second largest sugar factory in America. Sugar is big business in the Thumb.

According to legend, and Dorr Wiltse, a man named William Hoodless worked at the sugar factory in Caro and created a formula for a soft drink with some of his co-workers. In later years he became the President of Pennsylvania Sugar Refining Company where his formula was said to be used to create Pepsi! I guess he was the first of the "Pepsi Generation."

Perhaps the biggest and certainly the oldest event in Caro is the Tuscola County Fair, founded in 1881. The fair is held at the Fairgrounds every July. Don't miss the Caro 150 Snowmobile race and Winter fest in January and the Pumpkin Fest in October.

The Mystery of the Stained Glass

The Tuscola County Courthouse is a stately building in the middle of a courthouse square. It was Peter DeWitt Bush, Caro's second settler, who donated that property to the county for a courthouse in 1866. The first courthouse was an old church that Bush and neighbors moved to the site.

Tuscola County Courthouse

In 1873 the old church/courthouse was replaced with a brick building that was used till 1932 when it was replaced by the current Art Deco edifice which is a registered Michigan Historic Site.

The current Courthouse was designed by Detroit architect William H. Kuni who also designed the Alpena County Courthouse, which was added to the Michigan Register of Historic Sites in 1982 and listed on the National Register of Historic Places in 1996.

The Tuscola County Courthouse was built by local builder Cecil Kelly. In 1948, Kelly went into business with his brother in law Sheldon and nephew Shurley Wilsie to open Wilsie Kelly Chevrolet in Caro.

The courthouse is an imposing building faced with Indiana limestone. Its centerpiece on the exterior is the clock overlooking the main entrance, and the beautiful stained glass window at the top of the marble stairs in the back of the building.

The window was designed by A. Kay Herbert of Detroit and created by the Detroit Stained Glass Works, which was established at Detroit by Charles Friederichs and Peter Staffin in 1861. It closed in 1970 after more than a century of producing stained glass windows for churches, homes, steamboats and railroad cars in Michigan and beyond.

This window is said to show General Lewis Cass signing the Treaty of Saginaw with the Chippewa people in 1819 on the banks of the Cass River. The Treaty of Saginaw, as presented earlier in this book, transferred tribal lands to the United States.

The depiction shows General Cass and American soldiers on the left, Chief Joshua Maish-kee-awshe and his Chippewa braves on the right. The inscription says, "Gen. Lewis Cass signing an Indian Treaty along the banks of the Cass River."

However our historian friend, the late Dorr Wiltse Sr., thinks they got it wrong. He reminds us that the Treaty of Saginaw was signed in Saginaw! He suggests that this illustration is actually of the time Governor Cass did come to Caro.

Cass led an expedition to explore the Great Lakes and the Northwest Territory in 1820. Cass was known to have recruited the local Chippewas, who were expert canoe builders, to build the enormous canoes he would take on the trip. Wiltse says what the stained glass shows is a deal to build canoes for the Governor's expedition.

Whichever story the Tuscola County Courthouse's stained glass really does tell, it is a beautiful depiction.

Wahjamega

Wahjamega is an unincorporated community near Caro, just West on M-81. It was founded in 1853 by lumberman William A. Heartt. He was a major player in the lumber industry in the Thumb starting in about 1852. He was in the business for more than half a century.

To do business as a major lumber operation Heartt and his partners, James A. Montgomery, and Edgar George Avery, needed a post office, and a name for their community. So Mr. Heartt came up with an idea, he would take his initials, along with his partners, and create an acronym. William A. Heartt, James A. Montgomery and, Edgar G. Avery; Wahjamega.

Lumber was its first business, then farming and later the Michigan Farm Colony for Epileptics, now the Caro Center, was founded there. It was known as the Caro State Home. Today part of the facility is used as a prison.

Kingston

Kingston is a small town on M-46 a few miles east of M-24, in Tuscola County. The area's first settler was Alanson K. King in1857. It got a post office in 1867 as Newbury. But, since that was a name already used in the Upper Peninsula of Michigan, they were destined to make a change.

It is not known exactly when Newbury became Kingston, but we do know that the last time a plat was recorded in the area as Newbury was in 1891. Village records began to refer to Kingston in 1893, so that narrows it down.

Most believe that the town was named for Alanson King, the first settler and for one of the area's first postmasters, John Kingsbury.

Alanson King and his son Philo came to Kingston in 1857 built a log cabin and brought his wife. She said that after she moved to the area she didn't see another white woman for 6 months. He was from Massachusetts. Later Alanson's older brother John M. King came to Kingston. They were instrumental on the community's growth.

Not much is known about John Kingsbury except that he served as postmaster from 1863 to 1868. Alanson

King was also one of the first mail carriers, along with his son. In 1858 he began the route from Vassar to port Sanilac, a 70 trek that was often just a "blazed" trail. Kingsbury was succeeded by King's son Philo.

THUMB NOTE

In 1860 a farmer and hunter-trapper in Dayton Township (just west of Kingston) named Lyman Belknapp reported on his take in just two years.

He said he killed; 67 wolves, 104 bears and other wild game.

Back then when you planted your garden you had to keep an eye out for bear and wolves. Parents often had to take their kids to school because of the danger of them running into a bear on the way. Kingston and the Thumb were quite a wilderness.

The Kinston state Bank was founded in 1893 by Curtis MacPhail, of Cass City, the same Curtis MacPhail who has a son and grandson become members of the Baseball Hall of Fame.

THUMB NOTE

Kingston is also the birthplace of Michigan's 38th Governor, Murray Van Wagoner. Born in 1921 Van Wagoner earned a civil engineering degree from the University of Michigan. He is best remembered for his advocacy of the

Illustration by August Kimbrell

Mackinac Bridge. He was Oakland County drain commissioner, the Michigan Highway Commissioner and Governor from 1940-1942. During his term he, not surprisingly as a civil engineer, pushed road projects.

The Michigan Department of Transportation building in Lansing is named, the Murray Van Wagoner Transportation Building, in his honor.

Kingston has a connection with the world of race car drivers. Two of the fastest men alive in the early 20th Century got their start in Kingston, Bob Burman, and his younger Earl. They were both born in Imlay City, Bob in 1884 and Earl in 1899, and moved to Kingston with their parents where they grew up.

Governor Murray Van Wagoner

Speeding Through Kingston

Bob Burman set world records in his 200 horsepower Blitzen Benz racecar on the sands of Daytona Beach and at the first Indianapolis 500 in 1911. Before that, he won of the Prest-O-Lite Trophy Race in 1909. He was known as 'Wild Bob Burman" for his daring behind the wheel.

He was killed on April 8, 1916 in a race in Corona, California, when he rolled over in his open-cockpit Peugeot.

Three spectators were also killed, and five others

injured. At the time of his death he held 20 world records and held just been named "World's Speed King."

His death caused his friends Barney Oldfield, the first man to hit 60 miles per hour and Harry Arminius Miller to build a roll cage that completely enclosed the driver.

He was inducted in the National Sprint Car Hall of Fame in 2011.

His brother Earl Burman, another daring driver, met his end six years later at a road race at Santa Monica California. He was fatally injured

Bob Burman setting a speed record of 142 MPH in 1911. He sent this postcard to a relative in Flint and wrote on the back; "You see I can run other things besides restaurants." In Kingston he was a cook at Walter Legg's restaurant. Legg (10/2/1875-11/7/1961) was Author Michael J. Thorp's Great, Great Uncle.

during the Ford finals 5-mile race, when his car, traveling at a rate of 63 miles an hour, crashed into another machine piloted by R, J. Huebner, of Saginaw.

Bob and Earl Burman are both interred in Imlay City.

Vassar

Vassar is a beautiful little city right on the banks of the Cass River. In 1849 Townsend North and his brother in law James Edmunds arrived in the area. North owned 3,000 acres of wilderness, and lumber, along the river.

He got the land in payment for building the first bridge over the Cass River in Bridgeport.

They were looking for a place to build a dam and start a town. They found plenty of cork pine, a variety of white pine, and a great place to build. The trees were impressive, growing to a height of 150 feet, with diameters of more than three feet. Millions of board feet from Vassar and the Thumb would be marketed all over the world, especially in America's prairie states.

When lumber gave out, the local economy became more centered on agriculture, manufacturing, and commercial business.

The town was named for James Edmunds uncle, Mathew Vassar, the founder of Vassar College in New York State.

THUMB NOTE

Mathew Vassar was born in England in 1796 and immigrated with his parents to Poughkeepsie, NY. He made his fortune as a "masher of barley", better known as a brewer.

He was in his forties when his niece, Lydia Booth, suggested he consider establishing a women's college.

So, on February 26, 1861, the self-made man gave the college half of his fortune, $408,000, and 200 acres of land for the college. He was obviously a favored uncle!

He died in 1868 in a memorable way. He was giving his farewell address to trustees at the annual meeting of the board, he collapsed in mid-sentence.

He is remembered in a verse from a song that was popular at Vassar College.

"And so you see, to old V.C.
Our love shall never fail.

Full well we know that all we owe
To Matthew Vassar's ale."

Townsend North is considered the founder of Vassar. Born in Ulster County New York in 1814 North moved, with his father, to Washtenaw County, Michigan in 1835, where he was a carpenter. He was quite successful and is known to have built the first dormitory for the University of Michigan's new campus in Ann Arbor.

He moved to Flint in 1845, where he ran both a lumber yard and a hotel. In 1849 he founded Vassar. He built the T.N. North Bank in 1878, from bricks that were made in a kiln in Vassar.

By 1883 the bank became the First national Bank of Vassar. After 1926 the bank building was used for storage until in 1978 when it was moved to Genesee County's historic Crossroads Village where you can still see it and take a tour.

Chapter 8

Thumb Names

There are many little crossroads communities all over the Thumb to watch for. Some you can find on maps to this day, but are hard to find along the road. Some places the only thing left to mark a former community is a little sign along the road that marks a place; kind of ghost community; the imprint of the past. They started out as train stops, lumber camps, lumber mills, and post offices and sometimes they grew, and sometimes they all but disappeared.

Places like, Bach, Watrousville, Akron, Fairgrove, Mayville, Wilmot, Juniata, Ownedale, Gagetown, and Snover are still there.

Named For Postmaster-Relative-Friend-First Settler

Back then they were naming so many places that often they would name a place not only after the first settler, but also after the first Postmaster, John Kinde, the name of an uncle, Mathew Vassar or a business associate Leonard Case.

Names also came from the first settlers like the lumbermen who came to local areas to build mills and villages; people like; Aaron Watrous, John Wilmot, Joseph Gage, Frederick Bach, (not Johan Sebastian Bach) and Port Austin.

Made Up Names

Wahjamega, Tuscola and Caro aren't the only places with names that were just made up. Novesta Township was the last township to be organized in Tuscola County in 1869. There is a story about a group of settlers going to Caro, which was Centerville at the time, and talking around a potbellied stove at a store owned by a man named Farley Craw. When they told Craw they had to come up with a name he is supposed to have pointed to the stove, which was an Esta brand stove. On the stove was the label, "Esta No. V". He suggested they revers that name, thus was born Novesta Township.

Obscure Politicians

Communities, like Snover, were named for obscure politicians like Horace Greeley Snover. Snover was born in Romeo, Michigan, graduated from the University of Michigan Law School in 1871, became a judge and school principal in Port Austin. He served two terms in Congress, 1895-1899.

Fremont Township, Michigan is named for John C. Fremont, the man known as the "Pathfinder" for blazing the Oregon Trail. He ran for President in 1856, the first Republican candidate for President. He beat out Abraham Lincoln for the prize.

Dayton Township, Michigan is named for William

L. Dayton, a U.S. Senator from New Jersey. That's right, New Jersey! Dayton was also the U.S. Ambassador to France during the Civil War who worked to keep that country from recognizing the Confederacy. But that's not why the Township was named in his honor. He was the first Republican vice-presidential candidate, and ran on that ticket with Fremont. They were the anti-slavery candidates and lost the 1856 election to James Buchanan. People in Michigan were quite supportive of Fremont and Dayton.

Croswell is named for Charles Croswell, elected Governor of Michigan in 1877 and served till 1881.

THUMB NOTE

Governor Croswell was born in New York and came to Michigan at age 12 to live in Adrian. He has no connection to Croswell except he was the 17th Governor of Michigan.

He is remembered for being a law partner of Thomas Cooley, taking part in the formation of the Republican Party where he was Secretary of the convention held at Jackson, Michigan. The State House of Correction at Ionia and the Eastern Asylum for the Insane at Pontiac were opened, and the new capitol building at Lansing was finished during his administration.

Governor Charles Croswell

Former Homes and Remembered Family Names

Communities in the Thumb, and around Michigan, were named for families left behind, like Marlette where the story is that two local Irish women happened to have the same maiden name, Marlet. They carved the name on a log and in 1866 when Gordon Rudd was postmaster he added an "e" when he suggested the name.

Deford was named in honor of a great friend of Arthur Newton, who founded the community in 1884.

Settlers fondly remembered their former homes and were often quick to give their new homes the name of their former homes. Places like; Akron, Ohio and Sandusky, Ohio.

Traveling around the Thumb is part history lesson and part geography lesson.

Chapter 9

Thumb Ports; Austin to Hope

Port Austin-Garfield Inn

Now, let's get back on the Blue Water Highway in Port Austin at the Garfield Inn. It is listed as a National Historic Site and has been around since the 1850's. Its architecture is in the French Second Empire style and is rich in both architectural detail and history.

It is called the Garfield Inn because James A. Garfield, our 20th President, was a frequent guest of the original owners, Maria and Charles G. Learned, so President Garfield did sleep here.

The Garfield Inn in its early days

Charles Learned bought the place in 1857 with money earned from his involvement in constructing the Erie Canal. A native New Yorker, Charles G. Learned also helped build New York City's water-works system. In 1837, like many, Learned and his brother-in-law came to Michigan to purchase several thousand acres of pine land to make money in the lumber business. In 1839, Learned and his wife, Maria Raymond came to Port Austin and bought a house on three acres of land in Port Austin.

Meanwhile, Learned's pine land, now shorn of its trees, became a 2,000-acre farm where he prospered as an agriculturalist and dairy farmer. Things went well for Mr. Learned and his wife and they enlarged and updated the house.

In the 1860s Ohio congressman, later president, James A. Garfield, who was a close family friend of both Charles and Maria Learned became a frequent guest at their home. Legend has it that Congressman Garfield may have been an even closer friend of Maria than of Charles, there are some telling letters between the two. In fact, some suggest that he may have been smitten with her! We can only guess.

U.S. Rep. James A. Garfield

THUMB NOTE

James Abram Garfield was really a remarkable man. Born in 1831 he was the 20th President of the United States. He was the only President ever to be elected as a sitting member of the House of Representatives, serving for nine consecutive terms from the State of Ohio. Garfield was not wealthy; he was raised on an Ohio farm by his widowed mother and elder brother. He worked at many jobs to finance his higher education at Williams College, Massachusetts, where he graduated in 1856.

He served as a Major General in the Union Army during the American Civil War, and fought in the battles of Middle Creek, Shiloh and

Chickamauga. Garfield's presidency lasted just 200 days: from March 4, 1881, until his death on September 19, 1881, as a result of being shot by an assassin on July 2, 1881. Only William Henry Harrison's presidency, of 31 days, was shorter.

From 1931 to 1979 the house served as the Mayes Inn and Tower Hotel. It was listed on the National Register of Historic Places in 1984. Unfortunately The Garfield Inn is closed and for sale today. Hopefully the right person will decide the Inn needs another life.

The Bank-1884

Speaking of another life, "The Bank 1884" got one thanks to a couple who thought it would make a great restaurant.

In 1884 Richard Winsor and Horace Snover built a sturdy, fireproof bank to serve Port Austin. Fireproof was a big deal at that time, just a couple of years after the great Thumb Fires of 1881. The two-story red brick building was the center of Winsor and Snover's banking, real estate, and insurance business, and a center of business in the little community of Port Austin.

In 1894, former Michigan governor Albert E. Sleeper, whose park we read about earlier, purchased the building and established the new Port Austin State Bank. Over the years the building also housed the Port Austin Township Library, a dentist office, and a bicycle repair shop. In 1957, after 73 years, the Port Austin State Bank moved to its new location a block away leaving the building empty for the next 25 years.

Then in 1982, Tony & Marily Berry converted the old bank into a restaurant. The Bank 1884 Food & Spirits opened its door on July 18th, 1984, one hundred years after Winsor and Snover first opened their door to the same building. It is known today for its fine dining and historic atmosphere.

Pointe aux Barques

Pointe aux Barques is a private community and a small Township right at the tip of the Thumb. Some even call a rock that sticks out over Lake Huron the "Thumb nail". The Township of Pointe aux Barques in Huron County is one of the smallest in the State with only three sections, and had a population of 10 at the 2010 census.

The tip of the Thumb

The area was said to be sacred to the ancient natives, so later tribes didn't live there, leaving the tip of the Thumb to "the old ones" for over 1000 years. It is believed that a French priest named Claude Allouez, who arrived in 1665, and the many French traders and trappers who sailed or canoed the area named this point of land Pointe aux Barques because the rocky shoreline looked like the prows of ships tied up on the shore. It still looks like that!

In the 1880's the land was lumbered of thousands of white pine trees, some as high as 200 feet. The lumber was milled and shipped by rail and barge to Flint,

Detroit, Saginaw and Bay City. Once the land had been lumbered, the Pere Marquette Railroad thought about opening a resort in the area, since they already owned the land. In the end it wasn't the railroad but the president of the railroad, Stanford Crapo, who decided to make the investment. With the railroad's promotion Pointe aux Barques opened in 1896.

The private family community continues in its second century and includes 66 cottages on over 900 acres of property. The private, nine hole, Pointe aux Barques Golf Course opened in 1898 is one of the first, if not the first, golf course in Michigan and is one of the earliest in the country

Grindstone City

There's not much left of Grindstone City. The quarry is still there, and you can buy the largest ice cream cone in the Thumb, plus there are some beautiful views. One of the most interesting things to see is all the grindstones that mark driveways and walks in the area. As you drive through see how many you can find.

Spare grindstones at Grindstone City

In about 1834 Capt. Aaron Peer & James Duffey came to the area to start a grindstone quarry. The quarry, shipping and lumbering were big business and the population grew to be pretty large, for the tip of the Thumb.

The quarry business was good for many years. Grindstones were necessary in most kinds of manufacturing. Then, in 1893 a guy named Edward Atcheson invented Silicon carbide, also known as carborundum. It was this invention that killed the grindstone quarry business almost overnight. According to the National Inventors Hall of Fame, "without carborundum, the production of precision-ground, interchangeable metal parts would be practically impossible." Earlier in Acheson's career, he had had worked for Thomas Edison.

In 1880, Acheson helped in the development of the incandescent lamp at Edison's laboratories at Menlo Park, N.J.

Today there is hunting and fishing and many vacation homes in the area. Captain Morgan's is the place to eat, and the Grindstone City General Store has a monster ice cream cone.

Huron City

The first sawmill was built by Theodore Luce at the site of Huron City in 1837. It soon became a booming lumber center. In 1852 Luce sold it to a lumberman named Brakeman, and the place became, "Brakeman's." Four years later Mr. Langdon Hubbard bought the mill and the creek and spent the next 40 years developing the village himself, he called his town, "Willow Creek" until it finally became Huron City in 1861.

Then it was all destroyed by the first great Michigan wildfires in 1871. It was rebuilt and destroyed again in the even more terrible fire of 1881, and again, rebuilt.

But the lumber did run out, especially after the 1881 fire, and Huron City faded into memory, even the post office disappeared in 1905.

When the Great Fire of 1881 burned down his Huron City for the second time, Langdon Hubbard went back to work. As he surveyed the ruins of his property he is said to have commented, "Well the ground is left. The fire cannot take away the soil. I will build again."

He did. Langdon Hubbard rebuilt his store and also a flour mill, saw mill, shingle mill, blacksmith shop and other business enterprises of the village. He also rebuilt the post office, general store and a rooming house. He rebuilt the town so it was ready to go, but sadly most of the people had left. Huron City never was able to make a come-back to its former size or importance. But the story didn't end, it just got more interesting!

William Lyons Phelps

Another generation of the Hubbard family stepped up to make her mark on the little town. Mr. Hubbard's daughter, Annabelle, married a very famous scholar; Yale Professor of Literature William Lyons Phelps. This couple made Huron City their summer home for the next 40 years. Professor Phelps was also an ordained minister who became known throughout the world as a leading literary scholar, educator, author, book critic and preacher.

In the summer of 1922, the pastor of the Huron City Methodist Episcopal Church asked Professor Phelps to preach the following Sunday. He did and was as big a hit in the pulpit as he was in the Lecture Halls at Yale University.

His Sunday afternoon services began to attract huge numbers of people. So many came to hear him preach; that the little church was expanded twice, in 1925 and again in 1929, to accommodate the crowds of people. There were often as many as 800 and 1,000 people who attended services at the little church in the middle of nowhere at Huron City.

Pointe aux Barques Lifesaving Station

Today Huron City is a museum complex that includes the 11 buildings Mr. Hubbard re-built. Langdon Hubbard's descendants still keep the history alive by caring for the buildings.

The buildings include his home, the Seven Gables House, the Church, his General Store, the Community Inn, an old log cabin that was moved from the grindstone City area, (which is why it was not destroyed in the Great Fire of 1881) and the Life Saving Station and a boat that were brought to the location from the Pointe aux Barques lighthouse after the lifesaving station was closed.

The buildings are still there today, but I have never seen it open. You can wander around the site and look it over, and hope for the opportunity to tour the buildings, hopefully in the near future.

Port Hope

As you continue rolling south on the Blue Water Highway you come to beautiful Port Hope. It's such a lovely name; suggesting divine intervention and that is exactly the story behind this little town on Lake Huron.

The land around Port Hope had been set aside as bounties, or pensions, for veterans of the War of 1812. In 1851 Lexington resident William Stafford bought the first parcel of land. Later, in about 1857, with Dr. Reuben Diamond and William Southard he invested in buying up more forty-acre parcels from the government. Diamond Creek is named for Mr. Diamond.

Port Hope Chimney

As the story goes Southard and Stafford came to the area on a schooner. They couldn't get too close to shore because of a heavy storm, so they were dropped off quite a ways offshore. As they fought the storm, while rowing in from the schooner, they vowed that if they made it to shore, they would name the spot Port Hope. They did, and they did!

Stafford, who was quite the entrepreneur, began to open the area to lumbering and by 1858 his company dock was constructed and mills were in operation. The Port Hope Chimney was part of that, built in 1858 by John Getz. The community grew up around the lumber mill on the lake.

Twice, in 1871 and 1881, the mill, its docks and equipment and the belongings of the entire community went up in flames in the Great Fires in the Thumb. Both times the only thing left was this Chimney which still stands next to the lake. Both times the community rebuilt, but the lumber mill was not reconstructed after the fire of 1881.

The second Great Fire of 1881 destroyed the last of the trees, and farming became the focus of business. Stafford made some adjustments and built a flour mill, elevator and a new dock to replace the one lost in the fire.

That last piece of Stafford's lumber mill, the Port Hope Chimney, stands like a cemetery monument well off the road, next to Lake Huron near where the old mill's dock once stood. It is the last standing chimney in Michigan from the lumber era.

Port Hope was incorporated in 1887. It took many years, from 1882 to 1903, but finally with a push from the Port Hope Businessmen's Association and the Croswell Sugar Company the Flint & Pere Marquette Railroad finally extended its tracks from Harbor Beach in 1903, in 1904 the depot was built. Freight service to Port Hope continued till the 1970s. Today the Friends of the Port Hope Depot are working to move and restore the 1904 depot.

Chapter 10

Thumb Points East

Harbor Beach

The earliest settlers to this area arrived in 1837 and established a lumber camp and sawmill. By 1855 the settlement was called Barnettsville. As I wrote earlier about the Great Fires, to save themselves from the Great Thumb Fire of 1881 many local residents sought refuge in the water of the harbor.

After the Thumb Fire of 1881 the town was renamed Sand Beach.

Then in 1899, in a marketing move, the city fathers decided to change the name of the village from Sand Beach to Harbor Beach, because they didn't want to leave the impression that the area has nothing but sand. In 1910, Harbor Beach officially became a city.

Harbor Beach was a logging town. It drove the economy and growth. But in 1872, when the town was named a Harbor of Refuge for shipping on Lake Huron, the new growth industry in town became shipping and sailors. In 1873 the town built a breakwall to create a harbor, a real harbor of refuge. During the heyday of Lake Huron shipping, from 1877 to 1899, 50,000 ships took refuge in Harbor Beach during rough seas and bad weather.

So, how was Harbor Beach chosen as a Harbor of refuge? First, there was a need. There was no safe place for ships between Port Huron's Fort Gratiot Light and Pointe aux Barques; that's 115 miles of dangerous coast in bad weather. After several wrecks along that stretch of coast in the 1870s the government decided a harbor of refuge was needed.

A Board of Engineers was assembled in Detroit in 1871 with instructions to identify the best location for the new harbor; they focused on Sand Beach and Port Hope.

The decision was quite simple and economical; the Engineers said that 7,000 feet of breakwater would be required at Sand Beach, while it would take 10,000 at Port Hope. So Sand Beach won the day and the harbor, the largest man-made freshwater harbor in the world.

Look out into the harbor today and you'll see the Harbor Beach Lighthouse. It is a "sparkplug" style lighthouse located at the end of the north breakwall of the harbor. Sometimes known as a bug light, a sparkplug light gets its name from its shape; kind of short looking, with a three-story living area and the lantern on top.

In 1890 one of Michigan's most remarkable and able political figures was born in Harbor Beach, then Sand Beach, Frank Murphy.

THUMB NOTE

Justice Frank Murphy

The University of Michigan Law School Graduate, was Michigan's 35th Governor, from 1937-39. He was Governor when the United Automobile Workers began the historic sit-down strike at the General Motors' Flint plant.

When 27 people were injured in a battle with police, including 13 strikers with gunshot wounds, Murphy called out the National Guard to protect the workers, and refused to order the Guard's troops to suppress the strike. He mediated the agreement that put an end to the confrontation.

Governor Murphy also served as; a Detroit Recorder's Court Judge from 1923-30, Mayor of Detroit from 1930-33, the last Governor General of the Philippines from 1933-36, Attorney General of the United States from 1939-40, and was appointed an Associate Justice of the U.S Supreme Court by President Roosevelt in 1940.

He wrote one of the most famous dissenting opinions in the history of the Supreme Court in the Korematsu v. United States case. In it he protested the decision to hold persons of Japanese descent in camps during World War II. He sharply criticized the majority ruling as, "legalization of racism", the first time the word "racism" found its way into a Supreme Court opinion!

In 1949, Justice Frank Murphy died at fifty-nine at Henry Ford Hospital in Detroit. His remains are interred at Our Lady of Lake Huron Cemetery of Harbor Beach, Michigan.

Medal of Honor

Another celebrated Harbor Beach native was Major Louis Joseph "Lou" Sebille who was born in 1915. He attended Wayne State University in Detroit, Michigan and, after graduation, moved to Chicago, Illinois where he worked as a Master of Ceremonies at local clubs.

He became a fighter pilot in the Army Air Corps during World War II and later the United States Air Force during the Korean War. He rose to the rank of Major and was the first member of the Air Force to be awarded the Congressional Medal of Honor. He received the coveted award posthumously for his actions on August 5, 1950 in South Korea during the Battle of Pusan Perimeter.

White Rock

The famous White Rock

As you travel south on M-25 you could pass by White Rock without even noticing. There really isn't a town, just a few homes and a business or two, but it was once one of the larger towns in the Thumb and its location is famous for a rock in the lake that was known all over the world.

That rock, a large White Rock found offshore, was famous and sacred to the Natives who passed by on the lake for centuries, you can't miss it. The area started as a trading post in the early 1800s, by the 1830s a small village had grown and by 1859 they had their own post office.

White Rock, sometimes called White Rock City, was once one of the biggest towns in the area. It had a busy port and a lighthouse built in 1856. It was all destroyed in the Great Thumb Fire of 1871. The small community never came back.

Why was the With Rock in Lake Huron famous all over the world? It was a boundary marker for the 1807 Treaty of Detroit.

The Treaty of Detroit was the treaty between the United States and the Ottawa, Chippewa, Wyandot and Potawatomi Native American nations. It was signed in Detroit on November 17, 1807, by William Hull Governor of the Michigan Territory.

He was the only representative of the U.S. It was also signed by representatives of the various tribes.

The treaty was an agreement by the tribes to give up the southeastern part of the state but kept land north of the boundary for the Indians. As you can see by the map, the boundary went along the St. Clair River to the white rock, then west to a point in Shiawassee County then south.

Treaty of Detroit boundary map

The white rock is still visible today from a State of Michigan Roadside Park. The rock itself is now about 12 feet in circumference, but used to be larger, and is about a half mile out in Lake Huron.

There many legends regarding the rock, it is known to have been hit by lightning many times. One story that is told by Native Americans is about the white men who wanted to hold a square dance on the rock. The Indians warned that would not be a good idea as the spirits wouldn't like it. As the story is told they had a dance anyway, though one of them heeded the warning and watched from a distance. He watched as lightning struck and killed the entire dance party.

Is this a true story? I can't be sure, but it is an eerie testimonial to the power of legend and of a big white rock off shore in Lake Huron.

Forestville

Another very small community along the Blue Water Highway is Forestville. The name Forestville came from the town's number one product, timber. In 1858 a Capt. E.B Ward built the first sawmill, then, he built a hotel the next year. Soon Forestville had its own post office and by 1895 it had incorporated as the Village of Forestville.

In the 2010 census there were 136 residents in the community on the lake. It has no harbor, but it does boast a boat launch.

Richmondville

As much as I have looked there is little information on the little crossroads community of Richmondville. Like many places in the Thumb, it was founded as a lumber center. Everybody in the Thumb wanted to mine some of that pine wood gold. The first building built there was a store built in 1860 by Luce, Mason & Company, to supply lumber men and the industry. Mr. Benjamin F. Luce was also the postmaster in 1860. The post office operated until 1906.

Forester

The first settler in Forrester was Alanson Goodrich in 1849. Soon he was joined by Jacob Sharp who built and lived in the first house.

They came, once again, for the lumber and to farm. In 1852 the F.T. Smith Company built a general store to supply lumbermen. It was called Forrester, with two "r"s because it was in the middle of a forest. The second "r" was dropped officially in 1883, though the new, and proper, spelling had been used for a while at the local post office, which was operated from 1858 until 1907.

Port Sanilac

As we drive down the road to familiar places, and sometimes not so familiar places we watch for markers. Like when I was young and driving to visit my Grandparents near Kingston, MI. I would go down Barnes Road, just outside of Millington till I saw the old school house on the right; then I turned left on Sheridan Road. The old one room school was my marker.

We do the same thing on our Thumb Drive. For example we get to Port Austin and when we see the traffic light at the top of the town you know you turn south to get to Bad Axe, and you go straight to get to Pointe aux Barques. It works the same for sailors.

Sailing the Great Lakes, for many years, meant hugging the coast to get to where you were going. Ship captains stayed close to shore to; find their way, and stay as safe as possible from lake storms.

That's why we have accounts of all the fires that were burning in 1881 before the fires began to rage, ship captains were sailing the coast and saw it!

Just like drivers traveling down M-25, ship captains watched for markers along the way. Often those places that were markers, by land or water became the place names of local communities. Grand Rapids was a place where there were rapids in the river, Chesaning was the Indian word for big rock, (there was a big rock in the river, Flat Rock had smooth rocks in the river, Crystal Falls had, well, the crystal beauty of the falls, Pointe aux Barques was named, as I noted earlier, because of the shoreline rocks that looked like ships moored, and White Rock, named for big white rock; a marker that was used not only be captains but also by early natives.

I tell this story because Port Sanilac started out as a marker for passing sailors along the shore of Lake Huron. It was first called "Bark Shanty Point" for the crude bark shanty that had been built along the shore. It was used by some Detroiters to make shingles from the abundant pine trees that were lumbered in the area after the first sawmill was built in 1848.

By 1857 they changed the name to Port Sanilac after the County. Sanilac is another Native American word, likely Algonquin.

Two possibilities, first the Algonquin word "zngwak" means pine, which would have been a natural name for this center of the lumber industry. The other, some say stronger, possibility is that the county, and village, were named for Chief Sannilac, who was Wyandotte.

Port Sanilac Light

Look around the town of Port Sanilac, you'll find a great harbor, places to eat and explore, wineries, farm markets, museums, theater and tucked away in a neighborhood; the Port Sanilac Lighthouse It is privately owned and still used as an active navigational aid.

The Port Sanilac Light is about halfway between the Fort Gratiot Lighthouse at the south end of the lake and the Point Aux Barques Lighthouse at the tip of Michigan's Thumb. While the U.S. Lighthouse Board had wanted a lighthouse somewhere along this stretch of coastline starting in 1868, it wasn't until 1885 that Congress finally appropriated $20,000 to build the Port Sanilac Light.

There are only two lighthouses in Michigan with the Port Sanilac Light tower's octagonal shape and hourglass silhouette. The other is Ile Aux Galets, at the north end of Lake Michigan.

The Fourth Order Fresnel lens first lit in October of 1886…it is still used today. What is a Fresnel lens? You probably use one every day. They are in; auto headlights and taillights, solar collectors, overhead projectors, traffic lights and more.

Fresnel Lenses, pronounce it "freynell", were invented by a Frenchman named Augustin-Jean Fresnel to be used in Lighthouses. The higher the number the more power-ful the light: first order might be used in a flashlight, the 4th order Fresnel lens used in the Port Sanilac Light could be seen 17 miles out in the lake when powered by electricity, as it was beginning in 1924. It could be seen 13 miles out when lit with kerosene.

Port Sanilac's last Lighthouse keeper was a woman named Grace Holmes. She wasn't the first woman lighthouse keeper and not the last. Like most of them, she was the widow of a lighthouse keeper. Grace became keeper when her husband William died in 1926. When the light was wired for electricity in 1924 it was the beginning of the end for Grace as a Keeper. The lighthouse keeper's job was eliminated in 1928.

Lexington

Port Huron, as we will learn a little later in this book, is one of the oldest communities in the state, and region; founded in 1668.

But beautiful Lexington was the first settlement north of Port Huron. It took another 167 years, but in 1835 the first settlers arrived in Lexington.

Of course it wasn't called Lexington then. Like many places in the state it changed names over the years. It was first called Greenbush in 1838. In 1842 brothers Samuel and William Monroe bought the land and called it Monrovia. So, unlike Monroe, Michigan it was not named for President James Monroe. So at this time one part of town was Greenbush, the other Monrovia. Both parts of town became Lexington when they were awarded a post office in 1846.

It became Lexington in 1846 thanks to a suggestion from Reuben Diamond, the same Dr. Diamond who had invested in land in Port Hope, and whose name was given to a creek there. He came up with the name Lexington because of his wife's family in the east. Her cousin was the famous Ethan Allen, the revolutionary hero who fought at the Battle of Lexington.

THUMB NOTE

Ethan Allen, the revolutionary patriot not the furniture maker, was a farmer; businessman; land speculator; unsuccessful writer, and politician

He was born in the frontier of Connecticut but is regarded as a founder of the state of Vermont He took part, with Benedict Arnold, in the capture of Fort Ticonderoga early in the American Revolutionary War.

He was a leader of the famous "Green Mountain boys", a tough and troublesome group of mountain farmers and hunters. He led his gang in driving New York settlers out of the, "New Hampshire Grants," technically owned by New York but soon to become Vermont.

He and Benedict Arnold took Fort Ticonderoga from the British in 1775. A few months later he attempted to take Montreal, but failed and was captured. It was the guns of Ticonderoga that were transported through the wilderness by Henry Knox that led the British to abandon Boston to General Washington's Army.

While Ethan Allen was a very interesting man he was not entirely heroic, and not completely a patriot. After he was released by the British he returned to "The Grants" which by 1777 had declared independence from New York and the new United States as the Vermont Republic. Allen and others in tried to get Congress to recognize them as a state.

When that didn't work, because New York

was a powerful state, he joined in controversial negotiations with the British to make Vermont a British province.

He died in 1789 at age 51 in Burlington, Vermont Republic before it had become a state.

In 1840 a hotel built with native logs at the corner of what is now M-25 & M-90. It was destroyed by fire in 1859 and a new hotel was built the next year called the Cadillac House. It is still there, called the Cadillac House Restaurant and Pub.

The first of many sawmills was built in 1846. Lexington had three large docks on Lake Huron to handle the loading of lumber and wood products on the schooners bound for Detroit, Cleveland, and Chicago. They were among the many things throughout the Thumb the Great Fires of 1881 destroyed. They were never replaced.

Gov. Albert Sleeper was from Lexington and worked as a clerk in the Merchant store before he became the Michigan Governor in 1920. We learned about him earlier in this story.

Today Lexington is a beautiful lake town, with beaches and shopping, boating and fishing. Among the more recent additions to downtown Lexington check out the Old Town Hall Winery in downtown Lexington.

The winery is part of a new and growing trend of wineries, and micro-breweries in the Thumb. The Blue Water Winery & Vineyards, located near Carsonville, grows the grapes that make the wine in the breeze of Lake Huron. You can taste what they grow at the Old Town Winery in Lexington.

Chapter 11

South to the Blue Water Bridges

Lakeport

Lakeport has a very radical history, and I'm not referring to the folks who live there, details on that coming up.

What became Lakeport was first platted in 1837 by Jonas Titus, he called it Milwaukie City. He put his Milwaukie City at the mouth of a creek he aptly named Milwaukie Creek. After all that work he never recorded it, which means he never legally filed the documents, but, the creek is still called Milwaukee Creek, but now it is spelled with two "ee"s. It would be very interesting to know why, why two "ee"s, why Milwaukie City? Did he just like the name? And, why didn't he record his plat map?

In 1840 lumberman Jonathon Burtch arrived and set up shop, and lumber mills. He was also the area's first Township Supervisor, and Lexington sits in Burtch Township in St. Clair County, named for him. By 1853 another lumberman; B. C. Farrand, hired David Ward to re-plat the village.

He actually recorded his new village as Lakeport on August 30, 1858. Mr. Farrand was said to have named it Lakeport because it was so close to Lake Huron.

And now: the radicals in our midst, or at least in Lakeport's midst. The year is 1962; it was the very beginning of the peace movement in the United States. That movement would culminate in events like, the Democratic Convention in Chicago in 1968, and Woodstock in 1969. But in Lakeport, at what would later become Lakeport State Park, the Students for a Democratic Society met and issued the "Port Huron Statement", which became the manifesto of the movement.

A few dozen young men and women spent days and nights discussing a draft of that manifesto drafted by Tom Hayden. Editor of the University of Michigan paper, Michigan Daily, and already a recognized figure in Democratic politics and even at the White House, Hayden was a grandly talented wordsmith.

While only a few dozen young men and women attended the convention to discuss the 25,700 word statement, it was written mostly by Tom Hayden who was the Secretary of SDS. He also happened to be from Detroit, went to University of Michigan and was married to actress, and activist Jane Fonda.

Port Huron

We're now coming to the end of our "Thumb Drive", in Port Huron, where the businessmen of the Thumb thought that most people would start their trip.

Port Huron is the second oldest European settlement in Michigan, after Sault Ste. Marie. This great city started as Fort St. Joseph in 1668. It was built by the French explorer and soldier Daniel Duluth. Well, we English speaking people called him Daniel DuLuth, his real name was Daniel Greysolon, Sieur du Lhut. He signed his name duLut! He was the first Frenchman to see the headwaters of the Mississippi, he visited the area where his namesake city, Duluth, Minnesota, is now located, he built French fur trading posts in the Lake Superior country and at the site of the city of Thunder Bay, Ontario, among other places.

When he built Fort St. Joseph (Port Huron), in 1668, he had 50 men with him, whose job it was to keep English traders out of the upper lakes. The fort was abandoned in 1688, but in 1814, as the War of 1812 raged on, Fort Gratiot was built on the same site, once again to keep the British from getting into the lakes. It was named for Charles Gratiot, the engineer supervising its construction.

Gratiot was a member of the fourth graduating class from the Military Academy at West Point, the class of 1806.

As a Captain in the Corp of Engineers he assisted Alexander Macomb in constructing a fort in Charleston, South Carolina. As General, later President, William Henry Harrison's Chief Engineer in the War of 1812, Gratiot built Fort Meigs in Perrysburg, Ohio, to counter British attacks on American forts in the Northwest. He also took part in the famous "Battle of Mackinac Island" in 1814.

In an interesting historic note; Gratiot, by this time a General, was dismissed from his job in river, harbor, road, and fortification construction by President Martin

Van Buren in 1838, his replacement, First Lieutenant Robert E. Lee!

Fort Gratiot was manned until 1822, and then it was used, off and on, during the American Civil War and after, finally closed in 1895. Lucius Lyon built the Fort Gratiot Light just north of Fort Gratiot in 1829.

Lucius Lyon another important Michigan figure. He was a surveyor and engineer from Vermont. His first job in Michigan, in 1829 at the age of 29, was to rebuild the Fort Gratiot Lighthouse near old Fort Gratiot.

Later, from 1833 to 1834 he was the Michigan Territory's non-voting Delegate to Congress before Michigan became a state. In fact, it was Lucius Lyon who presented the petition requesting Michigan's admission into the Union; on December 11, 1833. It wasn't until 1837 that Congress acted on that petition.

The delay was partly about the dispute with Ohio over the Toledo Strip and partly because of opposition from southern states who didn't want to admit another free state. Lucius Lyon was Michigan's first Representative to Congress, our first U.S. Senator and the first to serve in both houses of Congress from Michigan.

If you go to Port Huron today be sure you head down to the St. Clair River and find Pine Grove Park. That is where the forts were. It is a wonderful place to view the bridges, watch freighters go by, enjoy a picnic or just watch the water and fish. Some even say that a few of the houses north of the park may have begun as officer's quarters.

Fort Gratiot Light

The Fort Gratiot Lighthouse is the oldest in Michigan. Photo by Cecil Johnson

The Fort Gratiot Lighthouse, as we mentioned, was built near the site of the two forts that had been constructed on the St. Clair River at the mouth of Lake Huron. It is the oldest lighthouse in Michigan and the second oldest on the Great Lakes. The first lighthouse in the area was built in 1825 it was located just about where the first Blue Water Bridge stands today. It wasn't built very well, or in a very good place, and after a storm it collapsed in 1828.

In 1829 Lucius Lyon came and rebuilt the lighthouse north of the fort. It is still there today, you can walk right up to it. It is still an active lighthouse with a green flashing light that can be seen for 17 miles.

Lightship Huron

Lightship Huron

Also right there at the Pine Grove Park you'll find the Lightship Huron. A light ship went where a lighthouse couldn't be built. A lightship could do anything a lighthouse could. The Huron had a steam fog horn, an acetylene torch light and even a hand bell. There were many lightships on the Great Lakes at one time, but the Lightship Huron was the last one on the lakes. She had served from 1935 until 1970.

She was given to the City of Port Huron in 1971 and given a place of honor at Pine Grove Park in 1972 as: "a tribute to her vigilance and in fond memory of a bygone era." In 1989 the HURON Lightship was designated a National Historic Landmark, the only lightship on the Great Lakes to get that honor.

She is unique from any other lightship in the Great Lakes, her hull is painted black. Since 1945 the Lightship Huron was the only lightship in service with a black hull. The reason why is a bit of sailor trivia. The story begins in 1936 when she was assigned to the southern part of Lake Huron near Port Huron.

The place was called the Port Huron Cut. She was painted black with the white lettering "HURON" on both sides because she was assigned the black buoy side, or left side of the entrance to the Lake Huron Cut. They just never painted her another color.

Grand Trunk Railroad Depot

There is a great railroad history in Port Huron. The Grand Trunk Railroad Depot is part of the Port Huron Museum. It is also near the Grand Trunk Western Railroad Tunnel.

The tunnel was opened in 1891 and connects Port Huron, Michigan with Sarnia, Canada. This international underwater railway tunnel was the first international tunnel anywhere in the world, and remains the oldest in operation.

The depot is a really cool place even as just a railroad museum, but it is much more than that. The Port Huron Railroad Depot is also where 12-year-old future inventor and entrepreneur Thomas Edison began his business career.

THUMB NOTE

Edison was born in Milan, Ohio, the youngest of seven children. He moved with his family in 1856. It was a tough life for Edison in Port Huron. In 1859, when the railroad first began its run to Detroit, Edison convinced the company to let him sell newspapers and candy on the daily trips.

He later began to print his own paper, "The Grand Trunk Herald."

It was a brilliant move for the boy who was later to found 14 companies including General Electric. He became known as, "The Wizard of Menlo Park" for his inventions including; the light bulb, movie cameras, sound recording and hundreds of other amazing discoveries. Edison held 1,093 US patents in his name, as well as many patents in the United Kingdom, France, and Germany.

In an interesting side note, Henry Ford, of automotive fame, was a friend and admirer of Edison; such a fan that the proper name of his Henry Ford Museum and Greenfield Village is "The Edison Institute." Mr. Ford is supposed to have convinced Edison's son Charles, to seal a test tube with air in the inventor's room shortly after his death, as a memento. A plaster death mask was also made. You can find both the mask and the tube containing the last breath of Thomas A. Edison at the Henry Ford Museum.

Blue Water Bridge

We come to the end of our Thumb Drive here at the famous Blue Water Bridge, where it all started. The ground breaking ceremony for the first Blue Water Bridge was held on June 23, 1937 in Port Huron. It opened on October 10, 1938.

It was at that time that the businessmen of the Thumb created the "Blue Water Highway Association." Their goal, as I wrote earlier, was to get people to go north on M-25, the Blue Water Highway, and get some travel and tourist business in their communities.

Look closely and see both of the Blue Water Bridges. The two bridges cross the St. Clair River and connect Port Huron, Michigan U.S.A, with Sarnia, Ontario Canada. Photo by Sarah Tripp Emino

The Blue Water Bridge is actually two bridges. The first span, a "cantilever truss" style bridge was opened in 1938 and has a total length of 6,187 feet.

As mentioned earlier; it was just after this bridge was completed in 1938 that businessmen in the Thumb created the Blue Water Highway Association, hoping to get tourists to turn north when they got to the U.S.

When the first span was first opened it included sidewalks! Those were removed in the 1980s to make room for another lane of traffic. Traffic continued to increase and even after eliminating the sidewalks, it was obvious another span was needed. So, a second bridge, a "tied-arch" style bridge, opened in 1997. It is slightly shorter than the first bridge with a total length of 6,109 feet.

The Blue Water Bridges are toll bridges that are jointly owned by Canada and the United States. The toll pays for maintenance of the spans.

The Blue Water Bridges are the second-busiest crossing between the United States and Canada, after the Ambassador Bridge at Detroit-Windsor.

Thumb 'N Home

We've gone all the way from Frankenmuth to Port Huron on our "Thumb Drive." I will spend some time in Port Huron, likely along the river to watch the ships and river traffic, then I guess I will head west on I-69 to get home.

But, I'd much rather do it again; just go back up north on M-25 toward Lexington and Port Sanilac and Port Austin. I promise you will want to do it again too. There is just so much to see and enjoy about Michigan's Thumb.

This is the way the Blue Water Businessmen thought people would start their trip into the Thumb; from Port Huron as they jumped off the Blue Water Bridge. I took the route backwards, but you can do it any way you like.

All you have to do is read the book backwards!

Bibliography & Acknowledgements

Walls of Flames. Gerard Schultz.1968 (cat. #68-56145)

Chart of the Burnt District of Michigan. Sgt. William O. Bailey-*Report of the Michigan Forest Fires of 1881.*

Portrait and Biographical Album of Sanilac County. Chicago, Ill., Chapman Brothers, 1884

Portrait and Biographical Album of Huron County. Chicago, Ill., Chapman Brothers, 1884

Fiery Trial. Judge James Lincoln, James Donahue, Historical Society of Michigan, 1984

Michigan on Fire. Betty Solders, Thunder Bay Press, 1997

History of the Great Fires in Chicago and the West. Rev. E.J. Goodspeed. 1871

Re-Thinking Michigan Indian History. LeBeau, Patrick Russell. Michigan State University. East Lansing, MI 2005

Indian Names in Michigan. Virgel Vogel. The University of Michigan Press, Ann Arbor, MI.1986

Michigan Native Peoples. Marcia Schonberg. Heinemann Library, Chicago, Illinois. 2004

Geography of Michigan. John A. Dorr Jr. and Donald F.

Eschman. University of Michigan Press. Ann Arbor, MI.1970

Vol. VIII Part II, Geographical Report on Huron County Michigan. Alfred Lane. Board of Geological Survey. 1900

A Drive Down Memory Lane: The Named Highways of Michigan. Leroy Barnett, PhD. The Priscilla Press Allegan Forest, Michigan 2004

Kingston, MI 1857-1982. Quasqui-Centennial, Kingston Historical Society, 1982 F.P. Horak Company, INC. Bay City, Michigan

Remembering Tuscola- A Pictorial History. Heritage House Publishing, Marceline, MO. 64658, Copyright 1992

Photos by Michael J. Thorp, the Archives of Michigan Robert S. Schiller and as attributed

Illustrations by August Kimbrell

Pointe aux Barques Lighthouse Society

Port Austin Area Historical Society.

Ella J. Thorp, proof reader extraordinaire

Made in the USA
Charleston, SC
22 December 2014